Communicating Skills

LEVEL 6

Third Edition

Dave Martin

NELSON

CONTENTS

UNIT	WORD SKILLS	LANGUAGE SKILLS		WRITING SKILLS			STUDY SKILLS
		Punctuation and Capitalization	Grammar and Usage	Sentence Construction	Paragraph Construction	Composition Construction	
1	1 Learning to Classify *1*		2 Nouns Are Naming Words *3*	3 Complete and Incomplete Sentences *4*			
2	4 Animal Names *5*	6 Using Capital Letters: Part 1 *7*	5 Common, Proper, and Collective Nouns *6*				7 Using Dictionary Entry Words *8*
3		9 Using Capital Letters: Part 2 *10*	11 Singular and Plural Nouns: Part 1 *12*		10 Organizing Ideas into Paragraphs *11*		8 Following the Guide Words *9*
4	14 Syllables and Stress *16*		12 Singular and Plural Nouns: Part 2 *13*		13 Topic Sentences Point the Way *14*		
5	18 Synonyms: Words with Similar Meanings *20*		17 Singular and Plural Nouns: Part 3 *19*		15 Checking for Paragraph Unity *17*		16 Using the Pronunciation Key *18*
6			19 Understanding Verbs: Part 1 *21*		20 Adding the Details *22*		21 Using a Thesaurus to Find More Exact Words *24*

UNITS 1–6 REVIEW *p. 25*

UNIT	WORD SKILLS	LANGUAGE SKILLS		WRITING SKILLS			STUDY SKILLS
		Punctuation and Capitalization	Grammar and Usage	Sentence Construction	Paragraph Construction	Composition Construction	
7		22 Using Commas with Dates and Addresses *27*	23 Understanding Verbs: Part 2 *28*	25 Subject and Predicate: Introduction *30*	24 Introduction to Editing *29*		
8		27 Using Commas with Series *32*		26 Subject and Predicate: Changing the Pattern *31*	28 Giving Directions *33*		29 One Word, Many Meanings *34*
9			30 Verb Tense *35*		33 Putting Ideas in Order *38*		31 Using a Table of Contents *36* 32 Using an Index *37*
10	35 Simile, Metaphor, and Personification *40*	34 Using Commas in Direct Address and with Interrupters *39*		36 Subject and Predicate: Compounds *42*			
11		38 Using Commas with Appositives *44*	40 Irregular Verbs: Part 1 *46*	39 Combining Ideas with Appositives *45*	37 Developing Paragraphs with Examples *43*		
12	43 Homonyms: The Sound-Alikes *50*		41 Irregular Verbs: Part 2 *47*		42 Explaining with Reasons *48*		

UNITS 7–12 REVIEW *p. 51*

UNIT	WORD SKILLS	LANGUAGE SKILLS		WRITING SKILLS			STUDY SKILLS
13	44 Antonyms Are Opposites *53*		45 Pronouns: Substitutes for Nouns *54* 46 Irregular Verbs: Part 3 *55*	47 Using Compounds to Combine Ideas *56*			

UNIT	WORD SKILLS	LANGUAGE SKILLS		WRITING SKILLS			STUDY SKILLS
		Punctuation and Capitalization	Grammar and Usage	Sentence Construction	Paragraph Construction	Composition Construction	
14	**48** Changing Meanings with Prefixes *57*	**51** Using Quotation Marks with Exact Words *60*	**49** Making Pronouns Agree *58* **50** Pronouns and Antecedents *59*				
15	**53** Prefixes Show Numbers *62* **54** More About Prefixes *63*	**52** Quotation Marks with Questions, Exclamations, and Imperatives *61*		**55** Making Nouns and Verbs Agree *64*			
16						**56** The Time Order of a Story *65* **57** Understanding Plot *66* **58** Writing a Story *68*	
17	**59** Homonym Hunt *69*			**60** Be Careful with Compounds *70* **61** Pronouns and Compound Subjects *71*	**62** Varying Verb Choice *72*		
18	**63** Words That Are Sometimes Confused *73*		**64** Adjectives Add Details *74*	**65** Choosing Adjectives Carefully *75*		**66** Editing to Eliminate Unnecessary Words *76*	

UNITS 13–18 REVIEW *p. 77*

UNIT	WORD SKILLS	LANGUAGE SKILLS		WRITING SKILLS			STUDY SKILLS
19	**67** More Confusing Words *79*	**69** Quotation Marks with Titles *82*				**68** Writing Conversations *80*	
20	**70** Words with Suffixes *83*		**71** Using Adverbs with Verbs *84*	**72** Adverbs Make the Meaning Clear *85* **73** Turning Adjectives into Adverbs *86*			
21	**77** Suffixes and Spelling: Part 1 *90*		**74** Finding Adverbs by Position *87* **76** Problems with *Good* and *Well 89*	**75** Using Verbs and Adverbs Effectively *88*			
22	**78** Suffixes and Spelling: Part 2 *91*	**79** The Apostrophe with Contractions *92* **80** The Apostrophe with Possessives *93*			**81** Writing Descriptive Paragraphs *94*		
23	**82** Suffixes and Spelling: Part 3 *97*	**86** Problems with Apostrophes *102*	**83** Making Comparisons *98* **84** Comparing Irregular Adjectives and Adverbs *100* **85** Using *Lie* and *Lay* Correctly *101*				

UNIT	WORD SKILLS	LANGUAGE SKILLS		WRITING SKILLS			STUDY SKILLS
		Punctuation and Capitalization	Grammar and Usage	Sentence Construction	Paragraph Construction	Composition Construction	
24			**87** Prepositions and Prepositional Phrases *103*		**88** Order in Descriptive Paragraphs *104*	**89** Writing a Business Letter *106* **90** Writing a Letter of Opinion *108*	
25			**91** Using Phrases to Make Nouns More Precise *109* **92** Using Adverb Phrases to Explain *When, Where,* and *How 110* **94** Using Pronouns Correctly: Part 1 *112*	**93** Combining Sentences with Prepositional Phrases *111*			
	UNITS 19–25 REVIEW *p. 113*						
26	**96** Our Latin and Greek Roots *116*		**95** Using Pronouns Correctly: Part 2 *115* **97** Part 3 *118*				
27			**98** More Practice Using Pronouns Correctly *119* **99** Using Coordinating Conjunctions to Join Equals *120*	**100** Writing Compound Sentences *121* **101** Learning to Use the Semicolon *122*			
28						**102** Report Writing: Gathering Information and Taking Notes *123* **103** Report Writing: Organizing the Report *124* **104** Report Writing: The Introduction and Conclusion *126*	
29			**106** Introducing Subordinating Conjunctions *128*			**105** Organizing a Bibliography *127*	
30	**109** Clichés: Is Your Language Worn Out? *131* **111** Homonym Crossword *133*		**107** Introduction to Dependent Clauses *129*	**108** Using Complex Sentences *130* **110** More Practice with Combining Sentences *132* **112** Correcting Run-on Sentences *134*			
	UNITS 26–30 REVIEW *p. 135*						
	Mini Thesaurus *137*						Index *140*

Exercise 1 (Word Skills)

Learning to Classify

Whenever you put things into groups according to a plan, you **classify** them. All the items that are alike are put into one group. For example, cars could be classified, or grouped, by colour or by make of car.

A. Animals can be classified in many different ways. Here are two possibilities. See whether you can think of three more ways.

1. large animals – small animals

2. warm-blooded animals – cold-blooded animals

3. _____

4. _____

5. _____

B. One way to classify animals is to put all those that live in the same place into one group. Using the headings in the chart, classify the animals listed in the box.

brown bear, leopard, zebra, shark, octopus, giraffe, boa constrictor, porcupine, ostrich, stingray, beaver, squirrel, kangaroo, parrot, killer whale, monkey

Animals of the Grasslands	Animals of the Forests	Animals of the Jungles	Animals of the Oceans
_____	_____	_____	_____
_____	_____	_____	_____
_____	_____	_____	_____
_____	_____	_____	_____

C. Suggest a way to classify each of the following topics:

EXAMPLE: The books in the school library ___fiction – nonfiction___

1. The students in your class

   _____

2. The food you eat

   _____

3. The programs you watch on television

   _____

D. Words can also be divided into groups. Read the following list of words carefully.

skin diver	swamp	is	battleship	slippery
but	bent	small	and	seashore
wildcat	slug	surfboard	sheep	dentist

1. We could classify these words in many different ways. Perhaps the easiest plan would be to put all those that begin with the letter *s* in one group.

   Words beginning with *s*   **Words beginning with other letters**

   _____   _____

   _____   _____

   _____   _____

   _____   _____

2. Notice that some of the words, such as *skin diver* and *wildcat,* are the names of things. This time classify the words by putting all the name words in one group. You will find nine of them.

   Naming words   **Other words**

   _____   _____

   _____   _____

   _____   _____

   _____   _____

Exercise 2 (Grammar and Usage)

Nouns Are Naming Words

Words that name people, animals, places, things, ideas, or feelings are called **nouns**.

> *EXAMPLE:* people: my **brother**, **John Franklin**, that **detective**, our **coach**
> animals: several **jellyfish**, **Snoopy**, a **shark**, a fat **caterpillar**
> places: the **bakery**, **Kelowna**, our **basement**, **Ontario**
> things: my **ballpoint**, a cold **winter**, the last **bus**, these **pickles**
> ideas or feelings: **beauty**, **joy**, **wisdom**, **happiness**, **loneliness**

A. Circle the nouns in the following sentences. The number in parentheses tells you how many nouns are in each sentence.

1. The firetrucks and the ambulance roared across the bridge and around the corner. (4)

2. Sophia dropped the camera into the river when the boat hit the dock. (5)

3. The skunk finished drinking the saucer of milk and crawled under the bed. (4)

4. All week the trapper searched the valley for the missing hunters. (4)

5. The train moved slowly into the station and stopped with a loud screech. (3)

6. For two hours the astronomer watched the strange red star through her powerful telescope. (4)

7. Under the sink the detective found a broken cup and a rusty fork. (4)

B. Add at least five nouns to each of these lists.

1. Things you might find in the kitchen, such as *forks, spoons, toaster*

   _____

2. Things you could hear, such as *wind, sirens, explosions*

   _____

3. Things you might use at school, such as *notebooks, pens, desks*

   _____

Exercise 3 (Sentence Construction)

Complete and Incomplete Sentences

A **sentence** is a group of words that makes sense by itself.

    EXAMPLE: *Our team scored the winning goal in the final minute.*

    A group of words that does not make sense by itself is called an **incomplete sentence,** or a **fragment.**

    EXAMPLE: *Scored the winning goal.*
                   Our team.

Add words to each of the fragments to make them into complete sentences.

1. If the shark attacks _____

   _____

2. Suddenly the car with the dented fender _____

   _____

3. The artist who painted the mural _____

   _____

4. Before we could move _____

   _____

5. Just before the bear reached the boys _____

   _____

6. As the camel caravan passed _____

   _____

7. Just before the tornado reached our

   house _____

   _____

   _____

   _____

Exercise 4 (Word Skills)

Animal Names

Our world is full of strange birds and animals with fascinating names. When you write about animals, you need to be aware that there are often special terms that are not the same for all kinds of animals.

The young of many animals have special names.

EXAMPLE *A baby frog is a tadpole.*

Complete the following sentences with words from the list below. Use your dictionary or an encyclopedia if necessary.

spat	calf	joey	foal	cygnet	hatchling
kit	tadpole	pup	cub	gosling	squab

1. A young whale is a

_____

2. A young skunk is a

_____

3. A young seal is a

_____

4. A young kangaroo is a

_____

5. A young bear is a

_____

6. A young oyster is a

_____

7. A young alligator is a

_____

8. A young horse is a

_____

9. A young swan is a

_____

10. A young goose is a

_____

11. A young pigeon is a

_____

12. A young frog is a

_____

Exercise 5 (Grammar and Usage)

Common, Proper, and Collective Nouns

A noun that names a particular person, animal, place, or thing is called a proper noun. Notice that proper nouns always start with capital letters.

EXAMPLE: *After crossing the **Atlantic, Columbus** landed at **San Salvador**.*

A noun that does not name a particular person, animal, place, or thing is called a **common noun**. A common noun does not have a capital letter unless it is the first word in a sentence.

EXAMPLE: *After crossing the **ocean**, the **explorer** landed on an **island**.*

A noun that names a *group* of persons, animals, places, or things is called a **collective noun**.

EXAMPLE: *The cowboys drove the **herd** of cattle across the river.*

A. Write a proper noun for each of these common nouns.

EXAMPLE: girl __Jennifer__

1. month _____   5. city   _____

2. teacher _____   6. continent _____

3. street _____   7. car   _____

4. country _____   8. language _____

B. Fill in the blank in each phrase with the correct collective noun from the list below. Use your dictionary if you are not sure of the answer.

grove	pack	flock	school	herd
team	class	litter	deck	pride

1. a _____ of turkeys   6. a _____ of puppies

2. a _____ of players   7. a _____ of wolves

3. a _____ of antelope   8. a _____ of students

4. a _____ of trees   9. a _____ of salmon

5. a _____ of lions   10. a _____ of cards

C. What animals would you see if you watched the following groups?

1. an aerie _____   2. a gaggle _____   3. a covey _____

Exercise 6 (Punctuation and Capitalization)

Using Capital Letters: Part 1

Each of the following proper nouns must start with a **capital,** or **upper-case,** letter:

The name of a person or an animal

EXAMPLE: Ashley, Carlos, Snoopy, Pegasus, Uncle Mike, Grandma Sanchez

The name of a place

EXAMPLE: South America, Italy, Moose Jaw, St. Lawrence River, Berkley Street

The names of days, months, and holidays (but not seasons of the year: spring, summer, fall, winter)

EXAMPLE: Friday, April, Hanukkah, Mother's Day

The names of schools, buildings, and structures

EXAMPLE: Miller Park School, West Edmonton Mall, Confederation Bridge

The names of organizations, companies, and stores

EXAMPLE: Little League, United Nations, Petro-Canada, Tim Hortons

Proofreading means finding and correcting mistakes in capitalization, punctuation, and spelling. Proofread the following sentences. Draw a line through each small, or lower-case, letter that should be a capital letter. Write the capital letter above it.

EXAMPLE: the city of fredericton, new brunswick, is on the saint john river.

1. erica attends maple creek middle school in borden, manitoba.

2. last july my uncle phil climbed mount fuji, the highest mountain in japan.

3. the final game will be played on st. patrick's day in ferguson arena.

4. last winter the boy scouts sold christmas trees in the parking lot on wilton avenue.

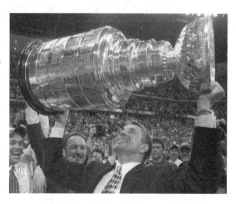

5. we saw the stanley cup when we visited the hockey hall of fame in toronto.

6. uncle farzeen works as a mechanic at adanac auto repairs on cambie street

Exercise 7 (Study Skills)
Using Dictionary Entry Words

The words listed in boldface type in a dictionary are called **entry words**. They are always arranged in alphabetical order. The information that the dictionary gives you about each word is called the **entry**.

To use a dictionary you must know the alphabet well. Putting words in alphabetical order is quite easy if they all begin with different letters. The job is harder, however, when they all start with the same letter. Then you must use the letters within each word to work out the correct order. First look at the second letter. If some of those are the same, look at the third letter, and so on.

Rewrite each group of words in alphabetical order.

EXAMPLE: cat, camel, carbon, calf, captain, cash, cave, candy

calf, camel, candy, captain, carbon, cash, cat, cave

1. largely, golf, jungle, heavy, furniture, magnet, idea, kidnap

2. adventure, awake, absent, agree, appear, act, afraid, alligator

3. make, middle, melody, milky, metal, magic, mercury, medium

4. pistol, pioneer, pink, pipe, pitch, pirate, pipeline, pinto

5. chisel, chimpanzee, chip, chimney, chipped, china, chipmunk, chin

Exercise 8 (Study Skills)
Following the Guide Words

At the top of each page in a dictionary are two words. These words are called **guide words**. The one on the left is the same as the first word on the page. The one on the right is the same as the last word on the page. When you are looking for a word in the dictionary, follow these guide words. Like signs on a highway, they tell you which way to turn to find your word.

A. Under each pair of guide words is a group of four words. Circle the two that belong on the same page as the given guide words.

1. snap – snow

   snug   snare   sneak   snake

2. tea – tent

   telegram   tear   taxi   tepee

3. girl – glide

   glad   globe   glider   glacier

4. dock – dollar

   dizzy   donkey   dog   doctor

5. rate – ray

   rat   rather   raw   rayon

6. march – mask

   mark   mast   marsh   marble

7. jug – junk

   juggle   jungle   just   Jupiter

8. pine – pistol

   pint   pirate   pin   piston

B. Sort the words in the box below into three lists. In List One put all the words that would be found on a dictionary page with the guide words **hardly** and **hash**. In List Two put the words that would be found on a page before **hardly** and **hash**. In List Three put the words that would be found on a page following **hardly** and **hash**. Each list should contain four words.

hatch	harbour	hate	hardware	harvest	handy
hammer	hay	harmful	hawk	harness	happy

List One	**List Two**	**List Three**
hardly – hash	**a previous page**	**a following page**
1. _____	1. _____	1. _____
2. _____	2. _____	2. _____
3. _____	3. _____	3. _____
4. _____	4. _____	4. _____

Exercise 9 (Punctuation and Capitalization)
Using Capital Letters: Part 2

Here are some more proper nouns that must start with capital letters.

The names of airplanes, ships, trains, airlines, and railroads

EXAMPLE: Boeing 747, Santa Maria, Air Canada

The names of languages and nationalities

EXAMPLE: Hebrew, Japanese, Greek, Swedish

The names of events or eras in history

EXAMPLE: World War I, the Middle Ages

The names of religions, gods and goddesses, and holy books

EXAMPLE: Buddhism, Shintoism, Shiva, God, the Qur'an, the Torah

Titles when they come in front of a person's name

EXAMPLE: Captain Anderson, Constable Chen, Doctor Kumar

The words *north*, *south*, *east*, and *west* are not capitalized when they name directions.

EXAMPLE: To get to the river walk east six blocks and then turn south.

These words need capital letters, however, when they name parts of the country or of the world.

EXAMPLE: Most of the world's oil comes from the Middle East.

Proofread the following sentences. Draw a line through each lower-case letter that should be a capital. Write the capital letter above it.

EXAMPLE: the chinese exchange students flew to london on british airways.

1. the town of hay river in the northwest territories is on the south shore of great slave lake.

2. most of the canadian swimmers are staying at the ideal motel.

3. the battle of the plains of abraham took place on september 13, 1759, southwest of quebec city.

4. the al rashid mosque in fort edmonton is the oldest mosque in canada.

Exercise 10 (Paragraph Construction)

Organizing Ideas into Paragraphs

A **paragraph** is a group of sentences that belong together because they are all about *one main idea*. Before you start writing a paragraph, brainstorm about the topic. (When you *brainstorm,* you try to think of several ideas that you will narrow down and organize later.) Then decide which part of the topic you want to use as the *main idea.*

A. Both of the following paragraphs are about starfish. As you read, think about which one has the more specific main idea.

> Starfish belong to a group of sea animals called *echinoderms.* The name means "spiny-skinned," and many of the animals in this group are covered with spines. These animals have no backbone. Besides starfish, the echinoderms include sea urchins, sand dollars, sea cucumbers, serpent stars, and sea lilies.

> Starfish feed in a peculiar way. The starfish can push its stomach out through its mouth. When it feeds on an oyster, it attaches its tube feet to the two halves of the oyster's shell and pulls the shell halves apart, opening a tiny crack between them. Then the starfish pushes its stomach, turned inside out, through the crack. The stomach surrounds the oyster's soft body, slowly digests it, and absorbs the food into the starfish's body.

1. What is the main idea of the first paragraph?

   _____

2. What is the main idea of the second paragraph?

   _____

3. Which main idea is more specific? Why?

   _____

B. Here are some paragraph topics. In your notebook brainstorm some ideas for each topic. Then write a main idea for a paragraph on each topic. Try to make each main idea as specific as you can.

EXAMPLE: Topic: Birds   Main idea: __Teaching a budgie to talk__

   1. Topic: Winter sports   Main idea: _____

   2. Topic: Dogs   Main idea: _____

   3. Topic: My family   Main idea: _____

Exercise 11 (Grammar and Usage)
Singular and Plural Nouns: Part 1

Nouns that name *only one* person, animal, place, or thing are called **singular nouns**.

    EXAMPLE: carpenter   hotel   boxcar

    Nouns that name *more than* one person, animal, place, or thing are called **plural nouns**.

    Here are some rules for making singular nouns plural.

    1. Most singular nouns can be made plural by adding -s.

    EXAMPLE: carpenters   hotels   boxcars

    2. Nouns that end in *s, x, z, ch,* and *sh* are hard to pronounce if only *-s* is added. To make these nouns plural, add *-es.*

    EXAMPLE: glass – glasses   box – boxes   bunch – bunches
                waltz – waltzes   bush – bushes

    3. Singular nouns that end in *y* are made plural in one of two ways:
        a. If a vowel comes before the *y*, simply add *s*.

    EXAMPLE: donkey – donkeys   holiday – holidays

        b. If a consonant comes before the *y*, change the *y* to *i* and add *-es.*

    EXAMPLE: city – cities   candy – candies

Make the following singular nouns plural.

Set 1		Set 2	
1. actress	_____	1. fox	_____
2. story	_____	2. valley	_____
3. alligator	_____	3. lawyer	_____
4. tax	_____	4. lily	_____
5. monkey	_____	5. walnut	_____
6. bathtub	_____	6. dish	_____
7. sky	_____	7. baby	_____
8. daisy	_____	8. army	_____
9. needle	_____	9. bench	_____
10. mattress	_____	10. donkey	_____

Exercise 12 (Grammar and Usage)

Singular and Plural Nouns: Part 2

Here are rules for nouns that end in *o, f,* or *fe.*
1. Nouns ending in *o*
    Many singular nouns that end in *o* are made plural by adding *-s.*

EXAMPLE: piano – pianos   radio – radios

Some singular nouns that end in *o* are made plural by adding *-es.*

EXAMPLE: potato – potatoes   mosquito – mosquitoes

A few nouns that end in *o* can be made plural by adding either *-s* or *-es.*

EXAMPLE: volcano – volcanos or volcanoes   zero – zeros or zeroes

2. Nouns ending in *f* or *fe*
    Some singular nouns that end in *f* or *fe* are made plural by adding *-s.*

EXAMPLE: cliff – cliffs   chief – chiefs

Other nouns that end in *f* or *fe* change the *f* or *fe* to *v* and add *-es.*

EXAMPLE: leaf – leaves   shelf – shelves

A few can be made plural either by adding *-s* or changing the *f* or *fe* to *v* and adding *-es.*

EXAMPLE: wharf – wharfs or wharves   dwarf – dwarfs or dwarves

Make each of the following singular nouns plural. Check those you are not sure of in your dictionary.

Set 1		Set 2	
1. hero	_____	1. wife	_____
2. burro	_____	2. tomato	_____
3. knife	_____	3. hoof	_____
4. scarf	_____	4. torpedo	_____
5. rodeo	_____	5. cuckoo	_____
6. calf	_____	6. roof	_____
7. cargo	_____	7. half	_____
8. handkerchief	_____	8. gulf	_____
9. giraffe	_____	9. avocado	_____

Exercise 13 (Paragraph Construction)

Topic Sentences Point the Way

Writers use a key sentence called a **topic sentence**. The topic sentence gives the paragraph's main idea and must catch the reader's interest. It must also tell what the paragraph is about. Often the topic sentence is the first sentence in the paragraph.

EXAMPLE: *The rings or circles on the Olympic flag have a special meaning.* The five circles stand for the five major continents of the world. To show that athletes at the games compete as friends, the rings are linked. The colours from left to right are blue, yellow, black, green, and red. They were chosen for a reason. The flag of every country in the world has at least one of these colours.

The topic sentence is printed in italics. Notice that the topic sentence quickly tells the reader the main idea of the paragraph.

A. In the topic sentence of the example paragraph we learned that this paragraph would be about the special meaning of the Olympic rings. What three meanings do the rings on the flag have?

1. _____

2. _____

3. _____

B. Here is a paragraph that does not have a topic sentence. Read the paragraph to find the main idea.

When you go cross-country skiing, sunglasses and sunblock are important to protect your eyes and skin from the sun's reflection off the snow. Snacks and water will help you from getting tired too quickly. A backpack is convenient to carry useful items you might need. It is good to take a cell phone in case of emergencies.

Circle the statement that best identifies the main idea of the paragraph.

The sun's reflection can be harmful

How to pack a backpack

What to take when you go cross-country skiing

C. Decide on a main idea for each of the following paragraph topics. Then use this idea to write an interesting topic sentence. Your sentence should tell the reader clearly what the paragraph will be about.

EXAMPLE: Topic: Things I could get along without

Main idea: _My younger brother's annoying habits_

Topic sentence: _Every day my younger brother invents new ways to upset me._

1. Topic: What I'd really enjoy doing

   Main idea: _____

   Topic sentence: _____

   _____

2. Topic: What our school needs most

   Main idea: _____

   Topic sentence: _____

   _____

3. Topic: A day I would like to forget

   Main idea: _____

   Topic sentence: _____

   _____

4. Topic: The best program on television

   Main idea: _____

   Topic sentence: _____

   _____

5. Topic: A character from fiction I would like to meet

   Main idea: _____

   Topic sentence: _____

   _____

UNIT 4

Exercise 14 (Word Skills)

Syllables and Stress

A **syllable** is a word or a part of a word that contains a vowel sound. A word has as many syllables as it has vowel sounds. Say the words *so*, *gate*, and *straight* to yourself. These words are one-syllable words because each contains only one vowel sound. Now say the word *tidy*. How many vowel sounds does it have? *Tidy* is a two-syllable word because it contains two vowel sounds (tī dē).

In words that have two or more syllables, one syllable is usually said with more force, or stress, than the others. Dictionaries mark the stressed syllables with a slanted line (´) called a stress mark or an accent mark.

EXAMPLE: *picnic (pik´ nik)   until (un til´)   elastic (i las´ tik)*

Say each of the following words carefully, listening for vowel sounds. Then write each word in syllables. Mark the syllable that is stressed with an accent mark. Use your dictionary to check your work.

EXAMPLE: dentist den´ tist

1. monkey _____

2. unpack _____

3. remember _____

4. punish _____

5. describe _____

6. terribly _____

7. twenty _____

8. discuss _____

9. piano _____

10. hiccup _____

11. pillow _____

12. laziness _____

13. mistake _____

14. unequal _____

15. inactive _____

16. pastry _____

17. invent _____

18. torpedo _____

19. lonely _____

20. explosive _____

21. kindergarten _____

22. difference _____

Exercise 15 (Paragraph Construction)
Checking for Paragraph Unity

Topic sentences are important because they hold a paragraph together. They explain what the paragraph will be about. When all the other sentences talk about the main idea in the topic sentence, the paragraph has **unity**.

When you write a paragraph, be sure to check for unity. Look at each sentence carefully. Ask yourself, "Does this sentence stick to the main idea in the topic sentence?" If one or more of your sentences talk about a different topic, your paragraph will not have unity.

A. As you read the following paragraph about fleas, check for unity.

Did you know that fleas are probably the best high jumpers in the insect world? In one experiment a flea jumped 130 times its own height. More than two thousand different kinds of fleas live in our world. Scientists have taken high-speed photographs of the flea's jump. The pictures show that the insect turns somersaults in midair, puts its legs over its head, and may even land on its target upside down.

1. Underline the topic sentence in this paragraph.

2. According to the topic sentence, what will be the main idea?

_____

3. Cross out the sentence that does not talk about the main idea.

B. Four of the following six sentences could be used in a paragraph about the discovery of diamonds in South Africa. Cross out the sentence that does not belong in the paragraph. Write **T** beside the sentence that you think should be the topic sentence. On the line below the sentences write the numbers of the other sentences in the order that makes the best sense.

1. Soon several more diamonds were dug up in the gravel along the river.

2. Almost one-half of the people in South Africa live in cities and towns.

3. On the banks of the Orange River they found an attractive stone.

4. In 1867 a group of children in South Africa made an important discovery.

5. Outsiders, hearing of these discoveries, began to pour into the area.

6. This pretty stone turned out to be a diamond worth $2500.

_____

Exercise 16 (Study Skills)

Using the Pronunciation Key

Often you will have to use your dictionary's **pronunciation key** to find out how a word is pronounced. A pronunciation key tells you how to pronounce the vowels and consonants in a word. This information is usually given in brackets right after each entry word. Sometimes the pronunciation looks the same as the spelling of the word.

   EXAMPLE: **bag** *(bag)*   **gasp** *(gasp)*   **rust** *(rust)*

With other words, however, the spelling and the pronunciation are quite different.

   EXAMPLE: **clay** *(klā)*   **comb** *(kōm)*   **night** *(nīt)*

Usually a complete pronunciation key is printed in the front of the dictionary. Most dictionaries also have a shorter form of the key on every second page.

In the box at the right is a pronunciation key from a dictionary. Using this key, write the regular spelling of each of the following words.

> cat, āte, fâre, fȧrm, mend, ēven, is, kīte, hot, ōld, ȯrange, cup, fûr, rūl. Use ə=a in about, e in under, i in pencil, o in lemon, u in circus

   EXAMPLE: rīt ____right____

1. trān   _____
2. ātē   _____
3. nīf   _____
4. rong   _____
5. nēdəl   _____
6. tuf   _____
7. diskrīb   _____
8. skāl   _____
9. ȯrgən   _____
10. letis   _____

11. brēz   _____
12. vənilə   _____
13. pōnē   _____
14. drū   _____

Exercise 17 (Grammar and Usage)

Singular and Plural Nouns: Part 3

A few nouns change their spelling when they become plural.

EXAMPLE: *goose – geese*   *man – men*   *child – children*

Some nouns have the same form in the singular and the plural. Most of these are the names of animals.

EXAMPLE: *deer – deer*   *sheep – sheep*   *aircraft – aircraft*

Write the plurals of each of these nouns. Then use your dictionary to see whether you are correct. Some of these words follow the rules you learned in Exercises 11 and 12.

Set 1

1. candy _____
2. tooth _____
3. tomato _____
4. box _____
5. moose _____
6. piano _____
7. life _____
8. mystery _____
9. kiss _____
10. monkey _____
11. blanket _____
12. foot _____
13. chief _____
14. echo _____
15. waltz _____
16. family _____
17. fireman _____
18. scratch _____

Set 2

1. solo _____
2. enemy _____
3. shelf _____
4. turkey _____
5. mouse _____
6. radish _____
7. country _____
8. hero _____
9. reef _____
10. chimney _____
11. volcano _____
12. fox _____
13. trout _____
14. leaf _____
15. march _____
16. butterfly _____
17. guess _____
18. potato _____

UNIT
5

Exercise 18 (Word Skills)

Synonyms: Words with Similar Meanings

Words that have the same meaning or almost the same meaning are called **synonyms**.

EXAMPLE: *strong – powerful   begin – start   tired – weary*

In this word search puzzle there are five synonyms for "small" and nine synonyms for "large." You can find them by reading down or across. When you find them, write them in the proper column.

W	A	B	L	B	L	I	T	T	L	E
N	M	I	M	M	E	N	S	E	O	P
D	I	G	I	A	N	T	S	A	P	G
E	N	O	R	M	O	U	S	T	H	R
F	I	X	F	M	A	S	S	I	V	E
O	A	B	S	O	Y	I	W	N	T	A
N	T	S	A	T	S	T	E	Y	E	T
A	U	O	D	H	U	G	E	E	E	D
G	R	A	J	U	M	B	O	T	N	A
S	E	M	L	T	V	A	S	T	Y	T

Small

1. _____
2. _____
3. _____
4. _____
5. _____

Large

1. _____
2. _____
3. _____
4. _____
5. _____
6. _____
7. _____
8. _____
9. _____

Exercise 19 (Grammar and Usage)

Understanding Verbs: Part 1

Nouns are words that name persons, animals, places, or things. **Verbs** are usually action words, such as *jump*, *crawl*, *shout*, or *stagger*. They explain what the nouns are doing.

> EXAMPLE: *Almost immediately the tiger* **attacked**.

Sometimes verbs explain what is happening in someone's mind.

> EXAMPLE: *Sergeant Pellizari* **recognized** *the car instantly.*
> *Mark and I* **studied** *science last night.*

Some verbs that we use all the time do not show action. These verbs tell us that something *is*, *was*, or *will be*.

> EXAMPLE: *Both Hannah and Sakina* **are** *in this race.*
> *My brother* **will be** *sixteen tomorrow.*

The most common nonaction verb is *be*. This verb has many different forms, such as *am, is, are, was, were, shall be, will be, have been, has been,* and *had been*. Remember that every sentence must have at least one verb.

Circle the verb in each sentence.

1. All night the young coyote searched for its mother.

2. Instantly the eagle pounced on the young rabbit.

3. We scrambled quickly to the top of the rocky slope.

4. The explosion rattled the windows in the cabin.

5. Last night I dreamed about a flight in a space ship.

6. Gradually the strange machine squeaked to a stop.

7. My sister and her friends were in the middle of the mud puddle.

8. Suddenly a large rock crashed through the kitchen window.

9. The first helicopter landed within five minutes.

10. Erica and Alex played chess until ten o'clock.

11. The two elephants collided with a tremendous thud.

12. Without a sound the snake slithered into the tall grass.

Exercise 20 (Paragraph Construction)

Adding the Details

As you have learned, the first step in writing a paragraph is thinking of a main idea. Once you have decided what you want to write about, the next step is to add information that explains or proves that main idea.

Remember that reference books are not the only places to get facts. You may be able to talk to someone who is an expert on your topic. Sometimes you may already know a great deal about the topic. The Internet is a good place to search for information.

A. Here is a paragraph about the shark's ability to smell. Notice how the author gives us a series of details that prove the main idea in the topic sentence.

Sharks have a keen sense of smell. They have been called hounds of the sea because they are able to follow a scent when they hunt. Their brains have been described as smelling organs because two-thirds of the brain's mass is used for smelling. A shark's sense of smell can be effective up to 100 metres from the source of the scent. The nostrils are never used for breathing but for picking up odours of fish, animals, and plants. Since a shark is able to detect one part of blood to 100 million parts of water, it is no surprise that a tiny drop of blood can attract sharks from a short distance away. Wounded prey brings them quickly, but sharks can also follow the scent of healthy fish.

List four details from the paragraph that show that the shark's sense of smell really is "keen."

1. _____

   _____

2. _____

   _____

3. _____

   _____

4. _____

   _____

B. Now it's your turn. Here is some information about the shark's enemies.

1. Other sharks – big sharks sometimes eat smaller sharks.
2. Porcupine fish – blow up like a balloon inside the shark's mouth. Spines dig into the shark's mouth and choke it.
3. Groups of porpoises – beat a shark to death by ramming into its body. Often damage the shark's gills so it is unable to breathe.
4. People – probably the most dangerous enemy. Humans kill millions of sharks every year.
5. Parasites – organisms that live on larger organisms and feed on them. A shark can have thousands of parasites living on its fins, tail, nose, gills, and eyes.

Write a paragraph using these details. Remember to give your paragraph unity by talking only about the shark's enemies. Use the following sentence as a topic sentence for your paragraph.

Although sharks do not have many enemies, there are a few animals

that can hunt and even kill them.

Exercise 21 (Study Skills)

Using a Thesaurus to Find More Exact Words

A **thesaurus** (thuh saw´ rus) is a dictionary of synonyms. The word *thesaurus* comes from a Greek word meaning "storehouse" or "treasure house."

In a thesaurus the entry words are printed in boldface type to make them easy to see and are listed in alphabetical order to make them easier to find. Each entry word is followed by a list of synonyms.

Get into the habit of using a thesaurus regularly to make your writing more specific. Synonyms seldom have exactly the same meaning. If you are not sure of the meaning of a word you find in a thesaurus, be sure to check your dictionary.

A. After each sentence, write at least three strong verbs that could replace the weak verb in boldface type. Use the mini-thesaurus at the back of this book for this exercise.

1. As soon as they lit the fuse, the men **moved** toward the shelter.

   _____

2. "Get out of here," **said** the police officer, "that gas tank could explode!"

   _____

3. All night the mountainous waves **hit** against the rocks.

   _____

4. Instantly the thief **took** the money and ran out the door.

   _____

B. These pairs of words are synonyms, but they do not have exactly the same meaning. On the line following each pair explain how they differ.

1. trunk, suitcase

   _____

2. bungalow, cabin

   _____

3. march, strut

   _____

A. Read the following sentences. Draw a line through each lower-case letter that should be a capital, and write the capital letter above it.

1. confederation bridge is about 13 km long and connects jourimain island, new brunswick, with borden-carleton, prince edward island.

2. how often have the winnipeg blue bombers won the grey cup?

3. constable nazar directed traffic at dawson road and carlton avenue.

4. mont-sainte-anne, near quebec city, is an important ski resort.

5. will forest view school have a valentine's day party?

6. in newfoundland we visited a viking settlement at l'anse aux meadows.

B. After reading this paragraph carefully, answer the questions that follow it.

Spiders use their silk for many different purposes. They spin some into webs to catch insects. Spiders spin a different kind of silk when making a cocoon to protect their eggs. The South American tarantulas are the world's largest spiders. The water spider builds a small silk tent at the bottom of a pond and fills the tent with air bubbles. Spiders even use silk when they travel. Wherever a spider goes, it spins a silk thread called a dragline behind it. If an enemy appears, the spider uses the dragline to drop from its web and hide in the grass. Once the danger is past, the spider climbs back up the dragline to its home.

1. Draw one line under the topic sentence in this paragraph.

2. What is the main idea of this paragraph?

    _____

3. List four details the writer gives to support this main idea.

    _____

    _____

    _____

    _____

4. Cross out the sentence in the paragraph that does not belong.

Review (continued)

C. Rewrite each group of words in alphabetical order.

1. ferry, fawn, flag, fence, fill, ferret, flipper, flat, fast

   _____

   _____

2. parrot, partner, parka, pass, past, partly, part, party, parade

   _____

   _____

3. scar, scarf, scare, scale, scarce, scalp, scatter, scary, scarlet

   _____

   _____

D. In the following sentences, circle all the verbs, underline the common nouns, and draw two lines under the proper nouns. Some sentences have more than one verb, common noun, or proper noun.

1. Millions of people watched the Olympics on television.

2. Brad climbed quickly up the steep hill.

3. Mom took our cat Sasha to the veterinarian.

4. Tom Watson reached Antler Creek on Tuesday.

5. Roula drove to the mall and bought groceries.

6. My sister baked a delicious pie.

7. The city of Montreal is on an island.

E. Write the plural form of each of these singular nouns.

1. loaf _____
2. guess _____
3. switch _____
4. bicycle _____
5. donkey _____
6. cod _____

7. mouse _____
8. story _____
9. chief _____
10. walnut _____
11. piano _____
12. child _____

Exercise 22 (Punctuation and Capitalization)

Using Commas with Dates and Addresses

In written language, punctuation marks help writers communicate clearly and precisely. Punctuation marks are like traffic signals. They tell the reader when to stop, when to go, and when to slow down or pause.

When you want to signal a pause, use a comma. The main job of the comma is to separate words that don't belong together.

1. Commas with addresses
When an address is part of a sentence, use commas to separate the city from the street. Commas must also be used to separate the province, state, or country from the rest of the sentence.

EXAMPLE: *You can write to Peter at 138 McDougall Street, Red Deer, Alberta T4R 1T5, until July 19.*

2. Commas with dates
With dates, separate the day of the month from the year with a comma. When a complete date is part of a sentence, separate the year from the rest of the sentence with a comma.

EXAMPLE: *Alexander Graham Bell was born on March 3, 1847, in Scotland.*

Add commas where necessary in the following sentences.

1. The small sailboat left Sydney Australia December 13 1997 and arrived in Wellington New Zealand on February 2 1998.

2. My pen pal lives at 784 Keffi Street Lagos Nigeria.

3. On Tuesday September 26 1989 the balloon landed near Belleville Ontario.

4. An earthquake in Bucharest Romania on March 4 1977 destroyed much of the city.

5. The flight from Dublin Ireland to Copenhagen Denmark took two hours.

6. Until Monday March 23 1998 her address was 2768 Claymount Road Clarksville.

7. My brother was born in Oslo Norway on June 6 1989.

8. At Planica Yugoslavia on March 14 1987 Piotr Fijas from Poland made the longest ski jump ever recorded.

Exercise 23 (Grammar and Usage)
Understanding Verbs: Part 2

Sometimes a verb is made up of more than one word. The verb parts that come before the main verb are called **helping verbs**.

> EXAMPLE: My uncle **is** flying to Hong Kong on Saturday.
> Martika and I **should** finish our project tomorrow.

Some sentences have two or three helping verbs before the main verb.

> EXAMPLE: The Edmonton Eskimo game **will be** played on Monday.
> The boat **should have been** painted yesterday.

Sometimes the helping verb and the main verb are separated by words that are not verbs.

> EXAMPLE: We **should** probably **have** brought rubber boots.
> He **had** not seen the jewels.

The following verbs are often used as helping verbs:

am	was	be	has	do	must	can	will	shall
is	were	been	have	does	may	could	would	should
are			had	did	might			

In the following sentences there are ten main verbs (one in each sentence) and fifteen helping verbs. Draw a circle around each main verb. Underline the helping verbs.

EXAMPLE: In a flash the fox <u>had</u> ⟨slipped⟩ under the fence.

1. The carpenters would have repaired the roof yesterday.

2. My grandfather was standing on the steps.

3. Your shoes will not be finished before five o'clock.

4. The snake must have wriggled farther back into the hollow tree.

5. The lock will probably open more easily now.

6. Within seconds the police had completely surrounded the building.

7. The apples under the tree were covered with wasps.

8. Several of the girls are not going to Glenwood tomorrow.

9. Those doors should have been locked before six o'clock.

10. An enormous pot was boiling on the stove.

Exercise 24 (Paragraph Construction)

Introduction to Editing

Editing, or revising, involves looking carefully at your written work and deciding how it could be improved. The word *revising* means "seeing again." Editing involves changing both *what* you said and *how* you said it.

Here is a checklist to use when you edit your work.

- Will my topic sentence catch the reader's attention? Can I improve it?
- Did I include enough details to support the main idea in the topic sentence?
- Do all the sentences belong in this paragraph?
- Did I present my ideas in an order that makes sense?
- Have I included any words or details that are not needed?

Use the editing checklist to revise the following paragraph.

(1) Robots are often used in dangerous situations. (2) One of the most dangerous environments where robots can work is on the ocean floor. (3) Jason Junior is an underwater robot that can dive to a depth of 61 000 metres. (4) This robot was used to explore the wreck of *RMS Titanic* and took pictures inside the ship. (5) The initials *RMS* stand for Royal Mail Ship. (6) Soon robots will be sent to Saturn. (7) Robots are also used for fighting dangerous fires. (8) They are especially useful with gasoline fires. (9) Unstaffed robots help scientists explore outer space. (10) In July 1997 a robot named *Pathfinder* landed on Mars.

1. Draw a line under the topic sentence of this paragraph. This topic could be more interesting. Rewrite the topic sentence to catch the reader's interest.

   _____

   _____

2. Draw a line through the sentence that does not belong in this paragraph.

3. Suppose you decide that you need more details. With further research, you discover robots are also used to fight chemical fires. Circle the number of the sentence to which you would add this detail.

4. Put an X through the number of the sentence in this paragraph that is out of order. Where do you think this sentence belongs?

5. The writer of this paragraph has overused the word *dangerous*. Use your thesaurus to find some suitable synonyms for this word.

6. In your notebook or on the computer, rewrite this paragraph, making the editing changes you have identified.

UNIT
7

Exercise 25 (Sentence Construction)

Subject and Predicate: Introduction

Sentences in English always have two parts. The first part, called the **subject,** tells who or what the sentence is about. The second part of the sentence is the **predicate.** It gives information about the subject or explains what the subject does.

Subject: Who or what is the sentence about?	Predicate: What do we learn about the subject?
The boa constrictor	is a large tropical snake.
The group of five clowns	arrived on a fire engine.

A. In each sentence draw one line under all the words in the subject. Draw two lines under all the words in the predicate. Every word in the sentence must be underlined.

EXAMPLE: Mario and Sean fired the cannon at exactly eight o'clock.

1. Great clouds of yellow smoke came from the top of the volcano.

2. The two girls scrambled down the rocky cliffs to the beach.

3. Several students from our school won a trip to Bermuda.

4. The large elephant held the log in place with its trunk.

5. Carmen and Alexis play for the school volleyball team.

B. Complete each of the following sentences by writing interesting predicates.

EXAMPLE: Several bits of wreckage from the raft

were scattered along the rocky coast.

1. Several of the lost hikers _____

_____

2. The huge bald wrestler _____

_____

3. Our neighbour, Hank Higgins, _____

_____

4. Hundreds and hundreds of beetles _____

_____

Exercise 26 (Sentence Construction)

Subject and Predicate: Changing the Pattern

The most common place for the subject is at the beginning of the sentence.

EXAMPLE: **A strange ticking noise** suddenly came from inside the box.

Always putting the subject first, however, is like having the same food for supper every day. All of us enjoy a change. To make your writing more interesting, try moving the subject sometimes. Subjects can be placed in the middle of the sentence.

EXAMPLE: Suddenly **a strange ticking noise** came from inside the box.

Sometimes you can put the subject after the predicate.

EXAMPLE: Suddenly from inside the box came **a strange ticking noise**.

A. In each of the following sentences draw one line under the subject. Draw two lines under the predicate.

EXAMPLE: The next day the five climbers crossed the glacier.

1. Instantly the two boys raced for the door of the cabin.

2. Just above the field mouse hovered a large hawk.

3. Without a word the stranger turned and disappeared into the darkness.

4. Early in the morning the lake is often covered with mist.

5. Right in the middle of the room sat a large skunk.

6. In the last fifty seconds our team scored three points.

B. Write sentences using these groups of words as subjects. Put the subject in the middle or at the end of each sentence. Each sentence should contain only one verb.

1. the pilot of the huge jumbo jet

_____

_____

2. my older sister's diary

_____

_____

UNIT
8

Exercise 27 (Punctuation and Capitalization)

Using Commas with Series

Events that happen one after the other or a number of similar things is called a **series**.

> *EXAMPLE: Out of the muddy water came a **series** of strange creatures.*
> *In October we played a **series** of games against the Mustangs.*

In language we often list a number of similar words in a series. Sometimes it is a series of verbs.

> *EXAMPLE: Caroline **shouted, screamed**, and **banged** on the heavy wooden door.*

The words in a series can be nouns.

> *EXAMPLE: Rabbits are hunted by **coyotes, foxes, mink**, and **weasels**.*

Sometimes the series is made up of groups of words.

> *EXAMPLE: Railroads use refrigerator cars to ship fresh meat and seafood, fresh fruit and vegetables, dairy products, and cut flowers.*

Notice that commas are used to separate the parts of a series. If you have a series of three items, you need two commas. If you have a series of four items, you need three commas, and so on.

A. In the following sentences underline the words or groups of words that are part of a series. Add commas where necessary.

1. Bobcats live in swamps woodlots deserts and rocky hillsides.

2. The large crowd clapped cheered and stamped their feet when Taylor scored the winning goal.

3. The stranger had broad shoulders powerful arms and huge hands.

B. Write sentences of your own using the following groups of words.

1. Andrea Jody and Ingrid _____

_____

2. over the rockslide through the creek and into the dense bush

_____

_____

Exercise 28 (Paragraph Construction)

Giving Directions

When you are giving directions, always make sure that they are *clear* and *accurate*. Remember to explain whether to turn left or right at intersections. Use compass points such as north, south, east, and west to make your directions easy to understand. If possible, mention well-known buildings, parks, and other important landmarks.

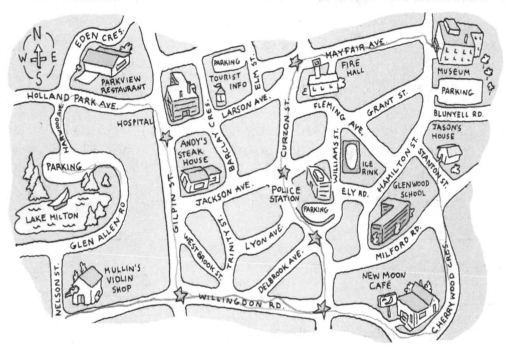

A. Here is a map of the city of Bloomfield. Intersections that have traffic lights are marked with the symbol ★. Jason Andrews lives on Stanton Street. One day he was riding his bicycle on Willingdon Road near Mullin's Violin Shop. A motorist stopped and wanted to know how to get to the museum. Read Jason's explanation carefully. Draw the route he suggested in pencil on the map.

Drive east on Willingdon Road until you reach the second set of traffic lights. Turn left and follow Curzon Street until you come to the third traffic light. Turn right on Mayfair Avenue. Go past the fire hall. The museum is at the end of that street.

B. Now imagine that you live in Bloomfield. Write a paragraph in your notebook explaining clearly how to make **one** of the following trips. Before you start draw a route on the map.

1. From Jason's house to the parking lot at Lake Milton.

2. From the corner of Larson Avenue and Barclay Crescent to the New Moon Café.

UNIT
8

Exercise 29 (Study Skills)

One Word, Many Meanings

Many words in English have more than one meaning. If you looked up the word *blind* in your dictionary, you would probably find an entry such as the one on the right. Eight different meanings of the word are listed. Often a definition is followed by a phrase or sentence in italics that shows how the word would be used with that meaning. In most dictionaries the more common definitions of the word are listed first.

> **blind** (blīnd) **1** not able to see: *The person with the white cane is blind.* **2** make unable to see: *The bright lights blinded me for a moment.* **3** without thought or good sense: *blind fury, a blind guess.* **4** take away the power to understand or judge: *His prejudices blinded him.* **5** done without the help of sight, using only instruments: *The pilot made a blind landing.* **6** a window covering, heavier and stiffer than a curtain, that can be closed by pulling it down or sideways. A **Venetian blind** is made of strips going across; a vertical blind has strips going up and down. **7** hard to see; hidden: *We were warned about the blind curve on the highway.* **8** hiding place for a hunter, wildlife photographer, etc. 1, 3, 5, 7 *adj.* 2, 4 *v.*, 6, 8, *n.*
> – **blind´ly**, *adv.* – **blind´ness**, *n.*

Look up the words in italics in the following sentences in your dictionary. Read all the definitions carefully. On the line below each sentence, write the meaning that makes sense in that particular sentence.

1. The dentist put a *crown* on one of my father's teeth.

   _____

2. Brandon's *aim* was to play shortstop for the Blue Jays.

   _____

3. My aunt has a large *bed* of daffodils and tulips.

   _____

4. Doctor Waldie *dressed* the wound on my brother's leg.

   _____

5. My sister plays in the *string* section of the school orchestra.

   _____

6. Early the next morning, Alison found the horses grazing in a *draw*.

   _____

7. In the *heart* of the forest, the escaped convicts felt safe.

   _____

8. The water-skier cut across the *wash* from the boat.

   _____

Exercise 30 (Grammar and Usage)

Verb Tense

In a sentence the verb is the action word that explains what the subject does.

>   EXAMPLE: *The large skunk* **marched** *into the principal's office.*

Verbs also tell us *when* the action happened. They have different forms to show whether the action takes place in the present, in the past, or in the future. The different forms of a verb are called **tenses**. The word *tense* means "time."

>   EXAMPLE: *Today the girls* **play** *Cedarville. (present tense)*
>   *Yesterday the boys* **played** *Pickford. (past tense)*
>   *Tomorrow both teams* **will play** *Kenton. (future tense)*

Forming the past tense of most verbs is not difficult if you remember these rules:

1. If the present tense ends in e, add -d.
   (*snore – snored*)
2. If the present tense does not end in e, add -ed
   (*cook – cooked*)
3. If the present tense ends in *y*, change the *y* to *i* and add -ed. (*carry – carried*)
4. If the present tense has only one vowel and ends in a single consonant, double the consonant before adding -ed. (*chop – chopped*)
   Verbs that form the past tense by adding -d or -ed are called **regular verbs**.

Write the past tense form of these regular verbs. In parentheses after each past tense form, write the number of the rule that you used to get the correct answer.

EXAMPLE: scurry <u>scurried (3)</u>

1. hunt _____
2. brag _____
3. smile _____
4. worry _____
5. drown _____
6. plan _____
7. arrive _____

8. cry _____
9. drop _____
10. save _____
11. shop _____
12. discover _____
13. hurry _____
14. snag _____

UNIT
9

Exercise 31 (Study Skills)

Using a Table of Contents

You will find the **table of contents** at the beginning of most nonfiction books. Its purpose is to give the reader an overview of what the book is about. Use the table of contents to quickly discover whether a particular book would be useful for the topic you are researching.

Contents

1. A Little Knowledge	1
2. Survival in the Sea	9
3. How Dolphins Communicate	13
4. Dolphin Family Life	21
5. How Dolphins Help Humans	27
6. How Humans Can Help Dolphins	35
Glossary	40
Bibliography	41
Index	42

In the box above is the table of contents for a book titled *Dolphins, What They Can Teach Us*, by Mary Cerullo.

1. In which chapter would you find information about why dolphins are ideally suited for life in the sea?

   _____

2. Where would you look to find out how dolphins "talk" to each other?

   _____

3. Which chapter would talk about ways to prevent dolphins from being caught in drift nets?

   _____

4. You may have heard that dolphins can be very helpful with children who are having serious problems learning to speak. Which chapter would probably have information on this topic?

   _____

5. Which chapter would tell you how the mother dolphin looks after her calf?

   _____

Exercise 32 (Study Skills)

Using an Index

An **index** is an alphabetical list of all the names and subjects mentioned in a book. The index tells the pages on which the topics appear. Indexes are usually found at the back of a book.

Following some headings, you may find the words *see also*. These words suggest other pages where you might find information about your topic.

In the box below is part of the index from a book called *Prairie Dogs*, by Dorothy Hinshaw Patent. Use this information to find the answers to the following questions.

1. On which pages would you find information on what prairie dogs eat?

   _____

2. Where would you find information on animals that hunt prairie dogs?

   _____

3. Prairie dogs are not members of the dog family. They are actually a kind of squirrel. Where would you find out how they got their name?

   _____

4. Which pages would tell you how many different kinds of prairie dog there are?

   _____

5. Where would you discover how prairie dogs help the grass to grow?

   _____

   _____

6. Which pages would tell you why cattle ranchers feel prairie dogs should be poisoned?

   _____

   _____

> prairie
>   disappearance of, 39
>   dogs (see also black-tailed
>   prairie dog)
>   decline in numbers of, 39
>   effect on grasses of, 42, 45–47
>   effect on prairie of, 49
>   feeding, 9, 29, 39–40
>   habitat of, 13–15
>   kinds of, 17
>   origin of name, 9
>   poisoning of, 40–42
>   predators of, 18, 19, 21, 37
>   size of, 11
>   tails of, 11
>   warning call of, 9
>   natural history of, 45–46
>   saving of, 56–57
>   types of, 14
> pronghorn antelope, 50, 51

UNIT
9

Exercise 33 (Paragraph Construction)

Putting Ideas in Order

When you tell someone how to do something, always arrange the steps in the order in which they should be done. This arrangement of details is called **time order,** or **chronological order.** The English word *chronological* comes from the Greek word *khronos,* which means time.

When you write instructions, it is helpful to use words and phrases such as *before you begin*, *the next step*, *then*, *after*, and *finally* at the beginning of some of your sentences. Expressions such as these tie your sentences together. Be sure, however, that you don't use a word such as *then* or *next* over and over.

A. Listed below in jumbled order are instructions for building a campfire. On the line below, list the numbers of the steps in time order.

1. Gather some tinder. Anything that will catch fire easily such as pine cones, dead grass, dried leaves, or pieces of bark can be used.
2. Light the tinder in several places with a match.
3. Scrape away the dry grass, leaves, and twigs, so that your fire will burn on bare earth.
4. Make sure no tree branches hang over the fire site.
5. Choose a sheltered place out of the wind.
6. As the flames build up, slowly add larger pieces of wood.
7. Place the tinder in the middle of the cleared area.
8. Arrange some branches about the size of a pencil like a tepee around the tinder.

5, 4, 3, 7, 1, 8, 2, 6

B. Once you have the directions for building a campfire in the right order, write a paragraph in your notebook explaining how to do it. Do not just recopy the directions printed in this book. Add words and phrases such as *before you begin, the next step, then, after,* and *finally*. Remember to start your paragraph with an interesting topic sentence.

Exercise 34 (Punctuation and Capitalization)

Using Commas in Direct Address and with Interrupters

When you speak to someone it is called **direct address**. A noun in direct address is set off from the rest of the sentence with a comma when it comes at the beginning or the end of the sentence. Use two commas when the noun is in the middle of the sentence.

> EXAMPLE: *Ming, did you bring your guitar?*
> *Are you sure, boys, that the door is locked?*

To help explain our ideas, we sometimes use words or phrases that do not affect the meaning of the sentence. These expressions are called **interrupters**. They may come at the beginning, middle, or end of a sentence. Interrupters must be set off from the other words in the sentence with commas.

> EXAMPLE: **By the way**, *the final game starts at eight o'clock.*
> *The team from Red Deer,* **on the other hand**, *arrived last night.*
> *The band from Fairmont will be here Tuesday,* **however**.

A. In the following sentences circle the nouns in direct address. Add commas where necessary. Remember that commas are also used with dates and words in a series.

1. Don't forget Pierre that school starts on Tuesday September 4.

2. Did you know that Mount Everest was first climbed on May 29 1953 Lee?

3. Michael please put apples oranges and grapes in that bowl.

B. Write sentences of your own using the following phrases as interrupters. Check your work by reading the sentences without the interrupter. The meaning of the sentence should not change.

EXAMPLE: as a matter of fact _Glen's turtle will probably win the race, as_

a matter of fact.

1. of course _____

_____

2. in my opinion _____

_____

UNIT
10

Exercise 35 (Word Skills)

Simile, Metaphor, and Personification

A good way to explain objects that are difficult to describe is to use **comparisons**. A comparison points out how things are alike and how they are different. Three imaginative ways to make comparisons are by **simile**, **metaphor**, and **personification**.

Comparisons using the words *like* or *as* are called **similes**. The word *simile* is from the Latin word *similes* meaning "like." In a simile two objects that are basically unlike but have something in common are compared.

EXAMPLE: *The wind last night was as cold as the dark side of the moon.*
From the plane, the town's streets looked like a giant checkerboard.

Metaphors are similar to similes except that they do not use the words *like* or *as*.

EXAMPLE: *The helicopter was an angry bee buzzing above the beach.*
(metaphor)
The helicopter buzzed above the beach like an angry bee. (simile)

In both sentences the helicopter is being compared to an angry bee. The first sentence is a metaphor. The second sentence is a simile because the writer used the word *like*.

To *personify* means "to make into a person." You use **personification** when you give something that is not human the abilities of a human being. Which noun is given human abilities in each of these sentences?

EXAMPLE: *The wind whispered through the leaves of the cottonwood trees.*
The old truck coughed as it slowly climbed the steep hill.

A. Complete each sentence with an imaginative simile of your own.

1. When he snored he sounded like _____

2. The canary was as noisy as _____

3. The cough syrup tasted like _____

4. After the hurricane the house looked like _____

5. Those cookies were as hard as _____

6. The baby guinea pig was as soft as _____

7. After running in three races, Ramaz was as tired as _____

8. When my brother plays the violin, it sounds like _____

B. Each of the following sentences contains a metaphor. On the line following each sentence, explain what two things are being compared and what they have in common.

1. Adrian rifled the hockey puck over the goalie's shoulder and into the net.

   _____

2. His face clouded over when he heard about the accident.

   _____

3. The hailstones were golf balls pounding down on the metal roof of the trailer.

   _____

4. The heavy snowfall blanketed the city.

   _____

C. In the blank at the end of each of these sentences tell whether the writer used a simile, a metaphor, or a personification. Be prepared to explain your answer.

1. The farmer watched the dust rise from his thirsty fields. _____

2. When my brother plays the violin it sounds like a dentist's drill. _____

3. The smokestack was a giant finger pointing at the darkening sky. _____

4. The searchlight stared into the foggy night.

   _____

5. A kangaroo bounded across the sand like an enormous jackrabbit. _____

6. The cannons thundered across the battlefield. _____

7. The fingers of the breeze ruffled Paulo's hair. _____

8. The wriggling fish were as slippery as wet soap. _____

UNIT
10

Exercise 36 (Sentence Construction)

Subject and Predicate: Compounds

A **conjunction** is a word that joins words or groups of words. The three most common conjunctions are *and*, *but*, and *or*. Sometimes conjunctions join two or more nouns to make a **compound subject**. The word *compound* means "having more than one part."

EXAMPLE: **Ravens** and **macaws** often live more than sixty years.

Conjunctions can also be used to join two or more verbs to make a **compound predicate**.

EXAMPLE: The macaw **screeched** angrily and **bit** the zoo-keeper's finger.

Fill in the blanks in the following sentences with interesting compound subjects or compound predicates.

1. _____ and _____ fed the goldfish yesterday.

2. In a flash the cat _____ across the kitchen and

   _____ on the mouse.

3. Furiously Ovid _____ the door and _____ down the stairs.

4. The _____ or the _____ will probably win first prize in the pet show.

5. Suddenly the large elephant _____ and _____ toward us.

6. The _____ and three _____ were injured in the explosion.

7. On the final turn, the racing car _____ and _____ into the fence.

8. At sunset the prisoners carefully _____ up the fire escape and _____ across the roof.

9. Some _____ and a large _____ live under the garage in the lane.

10. The daring hang-glider _____ off the cliff and _____ across the valley.

11. Natasha's _____ and _____ were missing when she opened her backpack.

Exercise 37 (Paragraph Construction)

Developing Paragraphs with Examples

Paragraphs can be put together, or **developed**, in a number of ways. When you are trying to decide how to organize your thoughts, always go back to the main idea of the paragraph. Then ask yourself these questions:
- What am I trying to do in this paragraph?
- What is the best way to make this idea clear to the reader?

Sometimes the best way to make your main idea clear is with a series of examples.

EXAMPLE: *Porcupines will chew on the strangest things. If you have a picnic in the woods, they will gnaw on anything you leave behind you. It is said that they can even chew through a glass bottle. Sometimes they get into a summer cabin that is closed up for the winter. There they may munch on old leather boots and aluminum pots. One porcupine even crunched up more than half a stick of dynamite!*

In this paragraph the main idea is clearly stated in the topic sentence: *Porcupines will chew on the strangest things*. In the sentences that follow, the writer gives specific examples of the strange things that porcupines chew.

Imagine that you live in the small town of Hickory Corners. The past winter was the coldest in Hickory Corners since 1924. You want to send an e-mail to a friend telling him or her how cold it was in your town.

1. Before you start writing, list four specific events to prove that the weather last winter really was unusual.

   _____   _____

   _____   _____

2. Many specific nouns can be used to describe winter weather. Some examples are *blizzards*, *frostbite*, *icicles*, and *sleet*. List at least five more specific nouns that you could use in your e-mail. Look up *cold* in a thesaurus.

   _____

3. Now list at least five verbs such as *shiver* and *chatter* that explain how people behave in extremely cold weather.

   _____

4. Now, using the ideas you have developed, write your e-mail on a computer or in your notebook. Pair up with a classmate and proofread each other's e-mail for spelling and punctuation.

Exercise 38 (Punctuation and Capitalization)

Using Commas with Appositives

A group of words that follows a noun and tells more about it is called an **appositive**.

> *EXAMPLE: Our dog, **a large German shepherd**, howled when the thunder began.*

The phrase *a large German shepherd* is an appositive. It gives us more information about the noun *dog*. Notice that appositives don't change the meaning of the sentence. Appositives are always set off from the rest of the sentence with commas.

A. Underline the appositive in each sentence. Draw an arrow from the appositive to the noun that it tells more about. Punctuate each sentence correctly.

1. Robert Munsch who lives in Guelph Ontario writes popular children's stories.

2. Jasper National Park the largest of the four Canadian Rocky Mountain Parks is 370 kilometres west of Edmonton.

3. We saw the *Bluenose* the ship pictured on the Canadian dime when we visited Nova Scotia.

4. Brandon the second largest city in Manitoba is on the Assiniboine River.

5. Lucy Maud Montgomery the author of *Anne of Green Gables* grew up in Prince Edward Island.

B. Choose four of the following topics. Write a sentence with an appositive about each topic you select. Remember to punctuate your sentences correctly.

Canada Day   hockey   my dog or cat   my father   my favourite author
apple pie   gophers   a mountain bike   my home town   a computer game

_____

_____

_____

_____

Exercise 39 (Sentence Construction)

Combining Ideas with Appositives

You can often use appositives to combine two sentences and avoid repeating information.

> *EXAMPLE:* *The surface of Mercury has many craters. Mercury is the closest*
> *planet to the Sun.*
> *The surface of Mercury, the closest planet to the Sun, has many*
> *craters.*

Combine each of the following sentences by making the second sentence into an appositive. Place the appositive directly after the noun it describes. Be sure to punctuate your sentences correctly.

EXAMPLE: Tokyo is one of the largest cities in the world. It is the capital of Japan.

Tokyo, the capital of Japan, is one of the largest cities

in the world.

1. Thailand is one of the world's main producers of tin. Thailand is a country in Southeast Asia.

   _____

   _____

2. Daniel Igali won the gold medal in wrestling in the 2000 Olympics. Daniel is a Canadian who was born in Nigeria.

   _____

   _____

   _____

3. The Sahara stretches across northern Africa. It is the world's largest desert.

   _____

   _____

4. Prince Edward Island is in the Gulf of St. Lawrence. It is Canada's smallest province.

   _____

   _____

Regular verbs add -d or -ed to make their past tense forms. A few verbs, however, do not follow this pattern. They are called **irregular verbs**. The **past participle** form of the verb is used after the helping verbs *has*, *have*, or *had*.

Present Tense (Today I)	Past Tense (Yesterday I)	Past Participle (Since last week I)
bring	brought	(have) brought
come	came	(have) come
do	did	(have) done
eat	ate	(have) eaten
give	gave	(have) given
go	went	(have) gone
see	saw	(have) seen
take	took	(have) taken

A. Complete each sentence with the correct form of the verb in parentheses. Remember to use the past participle after all the helping verbs.

1. The guinea pigs have _____ (eat) all their food.

2. Have you _____ (see) Courtney Roberts play goalie?

3. Jolene and I have often _____ (go) hiking in Manning Park.

4. Several of the boys had _____ (bring) their cameras.

5. Finally the mouse _____ (come) out from under the bathtub.

6. My sister had _____ (take) all the extra towels.

7. Richard had already _____ (do) most of the dishes.

B. Use each of the following verb forms correctly in a sentence.

1. has given _____

_____

2. went _____

_____

3. had eaten _____

_____

Exercise 41 (Grammar and Usage)

Irregular Verbs: Part 2

Here are more irregular verbs to learn.

Present Tense (Today I)	Past Tense (Yesterday I)	Past Participle (Since last week I)
begin	began	(have) begun
drink	drank	(have) drunk
ring	rang	(have) rung
run	ran	(have) run
sing	sang	(have) sung
sink	sank (or sunk)	(have) sunk
swim	swam	(have) swum

Complete each sentence with the correct form of the verb in parentheses. Remember to use the past participle after all helping verbs. Do not use the present tense.

1. Dylan and Kayla have not _____ (sing) that song before.

2. Before we reached Point Funston, the wind

   _____ (begin) to blow from the southeast.

3. The cat _____ (drink) the milk while we were out.

4. Probably the boat _____ (sink) during last night's storm.

5. Mario has often _____ (swim) across Whitefish Lake.

6. The bells in the tower had not _____ (ring) in ten years.

7. Before Haley could take the picture, the deer _____ (run) into the underbrush.

8. Has Zachary _____ (drink) all his chocolate milk?

9. The sheep had just _____ (begin) to enter the cave when Julie saw the wolf.

10. Within minutes the pirates had _____ (sink) the Spanish galleon.

Exercise 42 (Paragraph Construction)

Explaining with Reasons

When you write a paragraph that is developed with reasons, begin with a topic sentence that clearly states your main idea. Then present your ideas in a sensible order. Make sure that all your reasons support your main idea.

A. Scientists have suggested many reasons why the dinosaurs disappeared. Listed below are some facts about dinosaurs and their world. Check those that you think best explain why the dinosaurs died out. Choose the best order to discuss these facts. Then write the paragraph. Start with an interesting topic sentence that clearly states your main idea.

1. Dinosaurs ruled the earth for about 140 million years.
2. Dinosaurs did not hide or protect their eggs. Many eggs and young dinosaurs were probably eaten by mammals.
3. The climate became cooler and drier. Warm, wet jungles slowly changed to cool, dry forests.
4. When the climate changed, new and different kinds of plants began to grow. The plant-eating dinosaurs could not eat the new plants.
5. Some dinosaurs became so large it was hard for them to find enough food.
6. Dinosaurs need a warm, moist climate.
7. Like other reptiles, dinosaurs were cold-blooded.
8. When the plant-eating dinosaurs died out, the meat-eaters lost their main source of food.

_____

_____

_____

_____

_____

_____

_____

_____

_____

_____

Explaining with Reasons (continued)

B. Last July Brianna spent two weeks visiting her cousin Rachel in Lethbridge. Three weeks before Brianna arrived, Rachel's guinea pig had two babies. Brianna wanted to take one of the young guinea pigs home with her. She realized, however, that first she had to convince her parents that a guinea pig would make a good pet.

Because her parents lived some distance away, Brianna decided to write them a letter. Before she started, Brianna listed all the reasons she could think of why guinea pigs make ideal pets.

Here is her list.

1. do not need much room
2. can be raised on a simple diet
3. their food is not expensive
4. almost completely odourless
5. can be easily picked up and held
6. almost never bite

Using Brianna's ideas, write the letter to her parents.

_____

_____

_____

_____

_____

_____

_____

_____

_____

_____

_____

_____

Homonyms: The Sound-Alikes

Homonyms are words that sound alike but are spelled differently and have different meanings.

EXAMPLE: **meet** – **meat** are homonyms.

The word *homonym* comes from two Greek words, *homos* (same) and *onyma* (name).

A. Sometimes homonyms are used for humour. Circle the homonyms in the following limerick.

A flea and a fly in a flue,
Were imprisoned, so what could they do?
Said the flea, "Let us fly!"
Said the fly, "Let us flee!"
So they flew through a flaw in the flue.

B. For each of the following pairs of homonyms, write one sentence using both words.

EXAMPLE: fir – fur

Bits of rabbit fur were caught in the bark of the fir tree.

1. steal – steel

2. break – brake

3. coarse – course

4. threw – through

A. In each of the following sentences, underline the complete subject. Then rewrite the sentence, putting the subject in a different place.

1. The large crow flew across the clearing and through the open window.

   _____

   _____

2. The muskrats scrambled down the slope and into the pond.

   _____

   _____

3. The paramedics suddenly dashed into the smoke-filled building.

   _____

   _____

B. Combine each of the following pairs of sentences by making the second sentence into an appositive. Be sure to punctuate your sentences correctly.

1. Anders Celsius created his thermometer in 1742. He was a Swedish mathematician.

   _____

   _____

2. Venus is named after the goddess of beauty. It is the brightest planet visible from Earth.

   _____

   _____

3. Mount Logan is in Kluane National Park in Yukon. It is Canada's highest mountain.

   _____

   _____

Review (continued)

C. Add commas where they are needed in the following sentences.

1. My aunt's address after March 3 2003 will be 563 Fullham Road London England.

2. Gimli a town in Manitoba was settled by people from Iceland.

3. The rhinoceros eats grass leafy twigs and shrubs.

4. In my opinion Nadia you are the winner.

5. Vito of course will not be back until Friday August 4.

6. Ecuador a country on the west coast of South America exports large quantities of bananas cacao coffee rice and sugar cane.

D. Use each of the following verbs correctly in a sentence.

1. have run _____

_____

2. swam _____

_____

3. has drunk _____

_____

4. have done _____

_____

E. Say each of the following words carefully to yourself, listening for vowel sounds. Then write each word in syllables. Mark the stressed syllable with an accent mark.

1. potato _____   6. ignore _____

2. recognize _____   7. easy _____

3. lemonade _____   8. principal _____

4. antonym _____   9. careless _____

5. description _____   10. gymnasium _____

Exercise 44 (Word Skills)

Antonyms Are Opposites

Words that have opposite meanings are called antonyms.

  EXAMPLE: *rich – poor*   *strong – weak*   *sweet – bitter*

A. In each sentence fill in the blank with an antonym that rhymes with the word in italics.

EXAMPLE: Big is to *small* as short is to ____tall____

  1. Many is to *few* as false is to _____

  2. Fragile is to *strong* as right is to _____

  3. Hot is to *cold* as cowardly is to _____

  4. Bottom is to *top* as start is to _____

  5. Push is to *pull* as empty is to _____

  6. Dull is to *bright* as rude is to _____

  7. Float is to *sink* as grow is to _____

  8. Front is to *back* as tight is to _____

  9. Moist is to *dry* as low is to _____

  10. First is to *last* as slow is to _____

  11. Laugh is to *cry* as wet is to _____

  12. Good is to *bad* as happy is to _____

  13. Freeze is to *thaw* as cooked is to _____

  14. Whisper is to *shout* as believe is to _____

  15. Depart is to *arrive* as dead is to _____

  16. Expensive is to *cheap* as shallow is to _____

  17. Crooked is to *straight* as love is to _____

  18. Fresh is to *stale* as succeed is to _____

B. Using the same pattern, try writing two sentences of your own.

  _____ is to _____ as _____ is to _____

  _____ is to _____ as _____ is to _____

Pronouns: Substitutes for Nouns

A **pronoun** is a word that takes the place of a noun. The word *pronoun* is made up of *pro*, meaning "for," and *noun*. Words such as *I*, *you*, *they*, and *hers* are pronouns. By using pronouns, we can talk about someone or something without repeating the same noun.

> EXAMPLE: *Lauren's uncle promised that* **Lauren's uncle** *would take* **Lauren** *for a ride in* **Lauren's uncle's** *plane.*
> *Lauren's uncle promised that* **he** *would take* **her** *for a ride in* **his** *plane.*

Notice how the second sentence is much smoother and easier to understand.

The word that a pronoun stands for, or replaces, is called its **antecedent**. In this sentence the antecedent of the pronouns *he* and *his* is the noun *uncle*. The antecedent of the pronoun *her* is the noun *Lauren*.

List the pronouns in the following sentences. After each pronoun, write its antecedent.

EXAMPLE: During the game Jamie lost his watch. The referee returned it to him later.

it – watch   his – Jamie   him – Jamie

1. The ground squirrels darted for their burrows when they saw the coyote.

   _____

2. "Tiffany said she would come with me," replied Sarah.

   _____

3. Jacques got a bicycle for his birthday, but he can't ride it yet.

   _____

4. "Do you know where my books are?" asked Louise. "I put them on the window ledge," said Adam.

   _____

   _____

5. Leah left her project at school, but Tyler and Sergio took theirs home.

   _____

Exercise 46 (Grammar and Usage)

Irregular Verbs: Part 3

Still more irregular verbs to learn. (For others, see Exercises 40 and 41.)

Present Tense (Today I)	Past Tense (Yesterday I)	Past Participle (Since last week I)
break	broke	(have) broken
choose	chose	(have) chosen
freeze	froze	(have) frozen
speak	spoke	(have) spoken
tear	tore	(have) torn
wear	wore	(have) worn
blow	blew	(have) blown
grow	grew	(have) grown
know	knew	(have) known
throw	threw	(have) thrown

A. Complete each sentence with the correct form of the verb in parentheses. Remember to use the past participle after all helping verbs.

1. I've _____ (speak) to you before about throwing stones near those windows.

2. My parents have _____ (know) the Andersons for more than twenty years.

3. Bailey hasn't _____ (wear) her watch to school this week.

4. Several of the branches _____ (break) during the storm.

5. Has Ms. Simons _____ (choose) the winner of the contest?

6. After I had _____ (throw) the snowball, I saw Mr. Tanaka.

B. Write sentences of your own using each of the following verbs.

1. has blown _____

2. tore _____

3. have grown _____

4. froze _____

Using Compounds to Combine Ideas

In Exercise 36 you studied compound subjects and compound predicates. Often short sentences can be combined by using a compound subject or a compound predicate.

> *EXAMPLE:* *Rebecca enjoys playing ice hockey. Alexis likes playing ice hockey too.*
> *Rebecca and Alexis enjoy playing ice hockey.*

Combine each of the following pairs of sentences into one sentence with a compound subject or a compound predicate. Leave out any words that are unnecessary.

1. Regina is an important city in Saskatchewan. Another important city is Saskatoon.

   _____

   _____

2. The large owl suddenly swooped from the tree. It pounced on the young rabbit.

   _____

   _____

3. The large truck skidded on the ice. It crashed into the bridge.

   _____

   _____

4. Richard climbed Pinnacle Peak last Saturday. Gareth went with him.

   _____

   _____

5. The volcano destroyed many villages. It also killed 30 000 people.

   _____

   _____

   _____

Exercise 48 (Word Skills)
Changing Meanings with Prefixes

A **prefix** is a word part added to the beginning of a word to change its meaning.

Root Word	Prefix	New Word	New Meaning
certain	un-	uncertain	not certain
circle	semi-	semicircle	half a circle

The word *prefix* is made up of a Latin word meaning "to fasten" and the prefix *pre-* meaning "before."

Learning the meanings of common prefixes is important. This information will often help you figure out the meaning of a new word. For example, if you know that the prefix *mis-* means "bad" or "wrong," you would have no trouble understanding *misbehave* (behave badly) or *misspell* (spell incorrectly).

Here are three other commonly used prefixes:

Prefix	Meaning	Examples
re-	again, once more	reappear, recapture, rejoin, refit
pre-	before	prepaid, predict, prefix
trans-	across, over	transcontinental, transfusion

UNIT 14

Complete each sentence with one of the words listed below. Use each word only once.

rearrange	misuse	prearranged	repay	transplant
misplaced	preview	prehistoric	rebuild	misunderstood

1. The truck driver _____ our directions and took the wrong turn.

2. We had _____ to meet at the Park Motel at seven o'clock.

3. Fossils give us information about _____ times.

4. When we bought the new piano, we had to _____ the furniture.

5. Zinta had _____ her homework and couldn't find it in time for school.

6. When the ground warms up, my mother plans to _____ the cucumbers.

7. After the earthquake many people had to _____ their homes.

8. Cory and I went to a _____ of the movie last Thursday.

9. Tom plans to _____ the money he borrowed on Friday.

10. If you _____ your knife, it will soon become dull.

Making Pronouns Agree

Like nouns, pronouns can be either singular or plural. Here is a list of common pronouns. Notice that *you*, *your*, and *yours* may be either singular or plural.

	Singular Pronouns	**Plural Pronouns**
Person speaking	I, me, my, mine	we, us, our, ours
Person spoken to	you, your, yours	you, your, yours
Another person,		
place, or thing	he, him, his	they, them, their,
	she, her, hers	theirs
	it, its	

A pronoun must always **agree** with its antecedent. If the antecedent is singular, the pronoun must be singular. If the antecedent is plural, the pronoun must be plural.

> EXAMPLE: *The* **robber** *darted into the alley when* **he** *heard the sirens.*
> *The* **robbers** *darted into the alley when* **they** *heard the sirens.*

Be especially careful when the subject of a sentence uses *each*, *every*, or *one*. These words always take a singular pronoun.

> EXAMPLE: *Every house on the street had* **its** *windows broken.*
> *Each of the girls on the team should have* **her** *own key.*
> *Not one of the boys had remembered to bring* **his** *lunch.*

Fill the blanks with *he, she, her, his, their,* or *its*. Draw an arrow from the pronoun to its antecedent.

1. Will one of your friends let you use _____ jacket?

2. Every player on the team must look after _____ own uniform.

3. The students in Mr. MacNeil's class are having _____ party on Friday.

4. Before a member of the crew can go ashore, _____ must check out.

5. Every car in the parking lot had _____ window broken.

6. When the alarm sounded, every pilot knew what _____ had to do.

7. One of the girls on the relay team lost _____ shoe.

8. The members of the winning team will receive _____ ribbons.

9. Has each of the boys in the play learned _____ lines?

Exercise 50 (Grammar and Usage)

Pronouns and Antecedents

Pronouns must point clearly to the nouns they stand for. Read the following sentence carefully. Which girl do you think should leave?

Kim-An told Emily that she should leave immediately.

In this sentence the antecedent of the pronoun *she* could be either *Kim-An* or *Emily*. Often sentences with vague antecedents can be corrected in more than one way. Here are two ways to make the meaning of this sentence clear.

Kim-An said, "Emily, I should leave immediately."

Kim-An told Emily to leave immediately.

In the following sentences the reader may not be able to tell who or what the pronoun in boldface type refers to. Rewrite the sentences to make the meaning clear.

UNIT 14

1. As soon as the children got up from the tables, the janitor washed **them**.

   _____

   _____

   _____

   _____

2. My mother took the diamond necklace out of the box and gave **it** to my younger sister to play with.

   _____

   _____

   _____

3. Devin looked carefully at the man sitting across the table and then ate **his** hamburger.

   _____

   _____

4. Angela asked Melissa to look in **her** backpack.

   _____

   _____

Exercise 51 (Punctuation and Capitalization)

Using Quotation Marks with Exact Words

Use quotation marks when you want to show that you are writing the exact words that someone has said.

EXAMPLE: *"I must be home by ten o'clock," explained Christopher.*

Notice that quotation marks are used to mark the beginning and end of a quotation. The first word of a quotation always begins with an upper-case letter. Use a comma to separate the quotation from the rest of the sentence. If the quotation is at the beginning of the sentence, put the comma *inside* the second set of quotation marks.

EXAMPLE: *"My brother will be three next Tuesday," answered Jessica.*

If the quotation is at the end of the sentence, the comma goes *before* the first set of quotation marks.

EXAMPLE: *Instantly Sean replied, "I warned Roberto not to take the ring."*

Sometimes quotations are divided into two parts.

EXAMPLE: *"Let's wait until the rain stops," suggested Allison, "and then try to find the trail."*

When the quotation is divided, two sets of quotation marks are required. A capital letter is used only at the beginning of the quotation. Pay close attention to where the commas are placed.

In the following sentences underline the exact words of the speaker. Then punctuate the sentences correctly. Circle any letters that should be capitalized.

1. I want to speak to you snapped Mrs. Jawanda

2. please stop interrupting demanded the principal

3. go ahead whispered Tyler we're right behind you

4. you should be ready to play in six weeks the doctor told the injured hockey player if you follow my advice

5. if I were you insisted the officer I'd leave as quickly as possible

6. Gavin thought for a minute and then said the money is in my desk

7. we'll be all right answered Mr. Chambers unless the wind blows from the northeast

Exercise 52 (Punctuation and Capitalization)

Quotation Marks with Questions, Exclamations, and Imperatives

When a quotation is a question, an exclamation, or an imperative, be sure to punctuate the sentence correctly.

> EXAMPLE: *Mr. Whiteside asked, "Does this always work?"*
> *"Those hot wings are really spicy!" croaked Zoe.*
> *"Don't move!" shouted the officer suddenly.*

Notice that the question mark or exclamation mark is always placed *inside* the final pair of quotation marks. The question mark or exclamation mark takes the place of the comma if the quotation begins the sentence.

Punctuate these sentences correctly. Circle any letters that should be capitalized.

1. After staring at the floor for a while Juan said why did you do it

2. Arrest the man in the blue jacket the bank manager demanded

3. When are you planning to start asked the old soldier

4. Bring it here right now commanded the coach

5. But why asked Shelby did you not come earlier

6. Grab the rope and hold on shouted the paramedic

7. Can you get home by yourself asked the officer

8. Do you have any money asked Jody hopefully

9. I won't stay here alone all night shrieked Lynn

10. How did you know that demanded Seth

11. Lock that door immediately ordered the guard

12. But I didn't break that window insisted Mia

13. Are you planning to come with us asked Ming

14. Why weren't you here at ten o'clock snapped
    Ms. Bertuzzi

15. Come out from behind that box ordered the night watchman

16. Adrian studied the ring carefully and then asked where'd you find it

Prefixes Show Numbers

In 738 B.C.E. Romulus, the first ruler of Rome, introduced a new calendar. Instead of 365 days, his year had only 304. It was divided into ten months called *Marius, Aprilis, Maius, Junius, Quintilis, Sextilis, September, October, November,* and *December*. The last six names reflect the Roman words for five, six, seven, eight, nine, and ten.

We still use these ancient Roman numbers in many of our words. A *septet*, for example, is a group of seven musicians. A sea animal with eight arms is called an *octopus*. A period of ten years is a *decade*.

Here are some of the most common number prefixes in English.

Number	Prefix	Example
one	*uni-*	unicorn, unicycle
two	*bi-*	bicycle, biplane
three	*tri-*	triangle, trio
eight	*octa-, octo-*	octagon, octopus
ten	*dec-*	decade, decimal
hundred	*cent-*	centigrade, century

Use the number prefixes to do the following exercise. Use your dictionary and encyclopedia if necessary.

1. A three-legged stand used to hold a camera or a telescope is called a

   _____.

2. In 1967 Canada celebrated its one hundredth birthday, or

   _____. The United States became independent in 1776.

   In 1976 the United States observed its _____.

3. If you were having problems with a bicuspid, who would you go to see?

   _____

4. Most of us are *unilingual*. We use and understand only one language. A

   person who knows two languages would be _____. What

   would you call someone who speaks three languages? _____.

5. One event at the Olympic Games is the *decathlon*. Why is this event called a

   decathlon? _____.

6. To *bisect* means to divide into two equal
   parts. Using a ruler, *trisect* the rectangle at
   the right.

Exercise 54 (Word Skills)
More About Prefixes

Here are three commonly used prefixes.

trans-   means "across, over, down, or beyond"
sub-   means "under or below"
inter-   means "between or among"

Adding a prefix often makes a new word that is the **antonym**, or opposite, of the root word.

EXAMPLE: **un-** *(unlock)*   **in-** *(incorrect)*   **dis-** *(disagree).*

Before words beginning with the letters *m* or *p*, the spelling of the prefix *in-* changes to *im-*.

EXAMPLE: *possible – impossible*

A. Form the antonym of each word listed below by adding the prefix *un-*, *in-*, (*im-*), or *dis-*. Use your dictionary if you are not sure which prefix is correct.

EXAMPLE: certain _uncertain_

<table>
<tr><td>1. complete _____</td><td>7. patient _____</td></tr>
<tr><td>2. order   _____</td><td>8. fasten _____</td></tr>
<tr><td>3. honest   _____</td><td>9. visible _____</td></tr>
<tr><td>4. expensive_____</td><td>10. sane   _____</td></tr>
<tr><td>5. connect _____</td><td>11. prove _____</td></tr>
<tr><td>6. healthy _____</td><td>12. mature _____</td></tr>
</table>

B. Add either *trans-*, *sub-*, or *inter-* to each of these root words to create a new word. Use your dictionary to check your answers. Be sure you know the meaning of each new word you create.

1. school   _____
2. marine   _____
3. national   _____
4. form   _____
5. planetary   _____
6. plant   _____

Exercise 55 (Sentence Construction)
Making Nouns and Verbs Agree

In English, verbs and their subjects must always **agree**, or match. If the subject is singular, the verb must be singular. If the subject is plural, the verb must be plural.

> EXAMPLE: *That boy* **practises** *every day.*
> *Those boys* **practise** *only on Tuesday and Thursday.*

Notice that, unlike nouns, the singular form of the verb ends with an *s* when some third person (other than *you* or *I*) is the subject.

In most sentences the subject comes before the verb. If a sentence begins with *here* or *there*, however, the subject follows the verb. When you start a sentence with these words, always ask yourself, "Will the subject be singular or plural?" Use the verb form that agrees with the subject.

> EXAMPLE: *Here* **is** *the ring you lost.*
> *There* **were** *seven girls on the weightlifting team.*

The subject often follows the verb in questions too.

> EXAMPLE: **Have** *their suitcases been found?*
> *How often* **do** *those bells ring?*

A. Circle the form of the verb that agrees with each subject.

1. Kayla's gerbils (bites, bite).

4. Jennifer (giggles, giggle) constantly.

2. Our basement (leaks, leak).

5. Those players (appears, appear).

3. The buses (leaves, leave).

6. Their doorbell (rings, ring).

B. In each of the following sentences underline the noun that is the subject. Above the noun write **S** if the subject is singular, or **P** if it is plural. In the blank at the right write the form of the verb that agrees with the subject.

1. There (is, are) only five hot dogs left. _____

2. When (was, were) the jewels stolen? _____

3. Here (comes, come) the band from Langley. _____

4. How much water (does, do) that aquarium hold? _____

5. (Wasn't, Weren't) both drivers speeding? _____

6. (Hasn't, Haven't) those broken windows been repaired? _____

Exercise 56 (Composition Construction)

The Time Order of a Story

To write an interesting story requires careful planning. A good way to begin is to list all the events in the story from beginning to end. Be sure to arrange these events in the order in which they happened. This type of organization is called **time order**.

In ancient Greece one of the best-known storytellers was a man called Aesop. The following sentences, if arranged in the correct time order, retell one of Aesop's most famous stories, *The Tortoise and the Hare*. On the line at the end of the list, renumber the sentences in correct time order.

1. While the hare slept, the tortoise plodded on and on.

2. When the race began, the hare quickly outran the tortoise, who crawled slowly along.

3. The hare was always boasting of his speed in front of the other animals.

4. When the hare reached the finish line, he found that the tortoise had already won the race.

5. The hare thought this was a strange idea but agreed to the race.

6. Unfortunately the hare overslept.

7. Realizing he was far ahead, the hare lay down to rest and soon fell fast asleep.

8. One day the tortoise decided to challenge the hare to a race.

_____

UNIT
16

Exercise 57 (Composition Construction)

Understanding Plot

The plan of a story is called a **plot**. A good plot usually has four parts.

1. A beginning

Try to answer the "3 Ws." *Who* is the story about? *Where* and *when* does the story take place?

2. A problem

Someone or something that stands in the way of the main character

3. A struggle or conflict

What the main character does to solve the problem

4. A climax

The place in the story when the main character either reaches the goal or loses it completely

EXAMPLE: *As the sunlight slowly faded from the African plain, the hungry lioness caught her first glimpse of the zebra herd. Almost immediately her tail began to twitch rapidly from side to side. Her ears flattened as she crept slowly forward, hugging the dusty earth. The tawny yellow colour of her powerful body blended perfectly with the dried grasses of the plain. Whenever a zebra raised its head, the great cat flattened herself in the hot grass and remained motionless. Twenty minutes after the stalk began, she was within striking distance of one of the youngest members of the herd.*

Instantly the lioness rocketed out of the grass and raced toward her startled victim. Within seconds she leapt on the back of the fleeing animal, pushing its head down sharply with one paw. The young zebra pitched forward wildly and crashed to the ground in a cloud of dust. Moments later the struggle was over.

Understanding Plot (continued)

See whether you can find the four parts of the plot in the story on the opposite page.

1. Where and when does the story take place?

   _____

2. What does the lioness want? What problem must she solve to reach this goal?

   _____

   _____

3. List in order the five things the lioness did to catch the zebra.

   _____

   _____

   _____

   _____

   _____

4. What is the climax of the story?

   _____

   _____

5. Why did the author write this story in two paragraphs rather than one?

   _____

   _____

   _____

6. List five descriptive verbs that explain how the lioness moved.

   _____

   _____

   _____

   _____

   _____

Writing a Story

Remember that as well as plot and time order, a good story must have a topic sentence that catches the reader's attention. It must also use descriptive verbs and nouns and imaginative comparisons such as simile, metaphor, and personification.

Using the story of the lioness as a model, write a story of your own on the topic "a race I will never forget." Plan your story in two paragraphs. In the first paragraph describe what happens just before the race begins. In the second paragraph talk about the events leading up to the climax.

_____

_____

_____

_____

_____

_____

_____

_____

_____

_____

_____

_____

_____

_____

_____

_____

Homonym Hunt

Remember that homonyms are words that sound the same but have different meanings.

In the following exercise each definition is followed by an important homonym clue. Use this clue to help you find the missing homonym. Write the answer in the spaces at the right. Make sure each space contains only one letter.

1. A narrow strap used to guide a horse.

   It sounds like *rain*. __ __ __ __

2. A tube that carries blood to the heart.

   It sounds like *vain*. __ __ __ __

3. An animal hunted for food.

   It sounds like *pray*. __ __ __ __

4. The chair on which a king or a queen sits during ceremonies.

   It sounds like *thrown*. __ __ __ __ __ __

5. The bottom of a shoe. It sounds like *soul*. __ __ __ __

6. The hair around the neck of a lion. It sounds like *main*. __ __ __ __

7. People who are being cared for in a hospital.

   It sounds like *patience*. __ __ __ __ __ __ __ __

8. To change the colour of something. It sounds like *die*. __ __ __

9. To sail around from place to place. It sounds like *crews*. __ __ __ __ __ __

10. A smell left by an animal. It sounds like *sent*. __ __ __ __ __

11. A number of animals together. It sounds like *heard*. __ __ __ __

12. The part of a person's body between the ribs and the hips.

    It sounds like *waste*. __ __ __ __ __

13. A husky voice. It sounds like *horse*. __ __ __ __ __ __

14. A shower of frozen raindrops. It sounds like *hale*. __ __ __ __

Exercise 60 (Sentence Construction)

Be Careful with Compounds

The words *and*, *or*, *either* (with *or*), and *neither* (with *nor*) sometimes join two or more nouns or pronouns to make a **compound subject**. The word *compound* means "having more than one part."

> EXAMPLE: **Jenna, Kimberly,** *and* **Vanessa** *climbed Mount Reynolds on Saturday.*
> *Neither* **Adrian** *nor* **I** *likes peanut butter.*

When the subject is compound, it is often difficult to tell whether the verb should be singular or plural. Study the following rules and examples carefully.

1. When the parts are joined with *and*, a compound subject always takes a plural verb. Use a plural verb even if the subjects themselves are singular.

> EXAMPLE: **Lisa** *and* **Katy** *are always on time.*
> **Kangaroos** *and* **opossums** *raise their young in a pouch.*

2. When the parts are joined by *or*, *either* (with *or*), or *neither* (with *nor*)
   a. Use a singular verb if *or* or *nor* joins two singular subjects.

> EXAMPLE: *Neither* **Jesse** *nor* **Vince** *has won this race before.*

   b. Use a plural verb if *or* or *nor* joins two plural subjects.

> EXAMPLE: *Neither the* **trumpets** *nor the* **drums** *were damaged in the flood.*

Underline the compound subject in each of the following sentences. Write the correct verb form in the blank at the right.

1. Either Mr. Dempster or Amber (has, have) the key. _____

2. Both Stefan and Aaron (plays, play) on the school volleyball team. _____

3. Either the guinea pigs or the cats (is, are) always hungry. _____

4. Neither the cups nor the glasses (has, have) been washed. _____

5. Saskia and her brother (was, were) in the finals last year. _____

6. Usually either Alexandria or Imbi (helps, help) Simone clean out the aquarium. _____

7. Neither the high jumpers nor the pole vaulters (is, are) practising today. _____

8. The paperclips and the stapler (was, were) kept in that cupboard. _____

Exercise 61 (Sentence Construction)

Pronouns and Compound Subjects

Pronouns agree with compound subjects in the same way that verbs do.

1. Use a plural pronoun when two or more antecedents are joined by *and*. A plural pronoun is needed even if the antecedents themselves are singular.

EXAMPLE: *Suddenly the **lion** and the **tiger** escaped from their cages.*
*The **photographers** and the **reporters** ran for their lives.*

2. Use a singular pronoun when two or more singular antecedents are joined by *or*, *either* (with *or*), or *neither* (with *nor*).

EXAMPLE: *Either **Melissa** or **Perlita** should have her key.*

3. Use a plural pronoun when two or more plural antecedents are joined by *or*, *either* (with *or*), or *neither* (with *nor*).

EXAMPLE: *Neither the **coaches** nor the **players** had received their tickets.*

Circle the compound subjects in the following sentences. In each blank write a pronoun that will agree with the compound subject.

1. Either Richard or Nathan will bring _____ guitar.

2. Neither the raccoons nor the squirrels left _____ hiding places until the bear went away.

3. Ian and Po Lam will be given _____ awards by Miss MacRae.

4. Neither the hammer nor the chisel is where _____ should be.

5. Either Ursula, Amanda, or Carmelita will loan you _____ camera.

6. The boys and the girls left _____ uniforms on the bus.

7. Neither Latoya nor Brittany had finished _____ art project.

8. Austin, Blake, and Justin forgot to bring _____ lunches.

9. Nina and Zoe wore the shirts _____ had made at school.

10. Shui Ling and Jeremy rode _____ bicycles around Bonacord Park on Saturday afternoon.

11. Neither Jacques nor Ben could find _____ socks.

12. Either Noriko or Abigail forgot to take _____ sweater.

Exercise 62 (Paragraph Construction)

Varying Verb Choice

Our language is full of interesting verbs that explain exactly how someone moves.

> EXAMPLE: *A skier going down a hill might* **twist, turn, stumble,** *or* **tumble.**
> *An injured hiker could* **limp, stagger, stumble,** *or* **crawl.**

In the following paragraph the author has used the verb *went* in every sentence but the last. Rewrite the paragraph. Whenever you come to *went*, use another verb to explain exactly how the people in the story moved.

Well before sunrise the old prospector went silently across the small cabin and shook Ian. Once he was sure the boy was awake, he went to the stove to prepare breakfast. Later they went down the narrow trail to the lake. The old man and the boy went across to the far shore. After hiding the boat, the two went slowly along the banks of an icy stream until they reached the cliff. During the next forty-five minutes they went carefully up the slippery rocks. At the top, the old man rested while Ian went back to get the rest of their equipment. Then they went slowly through the thick forest until they reached a low cave. On all fours Ian went cautiously inside. Suddenly he saw it!

_____

_____

_____

_____

_____

_____

_____

_____

_____

Exercise 63 (Word Skills)
Words That Are Sometimes Confused

In English some pairs of words are confusing because they look and sound similar. You may already have learned some of these problem words. Study carefully those you are not sure of.

1. **accept**	to take or receive	Did you *accept* the money?
except	other than, but	Everyone left *except* Diane.
2. **advice**	helpful suggestions	We thanked Terry for his *advice*.
advise	to give advice	I would *advise* you to go.
3. **all ready**	completely ready	Supper is *all ready*.
already	by this time	Have they left *already*?
4. **all together**	all in one place	The glasses are *all together* on the shelf.
altogether	all included	There are several of us *altogether*.
5. **cloths**	pieces of fabric	Use those *cloths* to polish the car.
clothes	coverings for the body	Be sure to hang up your *clothes*.

Ten of the following sentences contain an error. Cross out the incorrect word and write your corrections directly above it. Put a check mark (✓) in front of the three correct sentences.

1. All of the girls are going accept Kathryn.

2. That box is all ready full.

3. Did Ms. Tanchuk advise you to come?

4. Next Saturday I can wear my new cloths.

5. All together there are seven mistakes.

6. Where did you leave the table clothes?

7. Everyone except Alex went home.

8. The three girls decided to enter the cave altogether.

9. Is the team from Boundary Bay School already to leave?

10. Be sure to follow the doctor's advise.

11. Which cloths should I use to wipe up the oil?

12. All the boys went swimming accept Aidan.

13. What did Mr. Goldberg advice you to do?

UNIT
18

Adjectives Add Details

Adjectives help give a clear picture of what you are describing. Notice how the adjectives in boldface type make the original sentence come to life.

> EXAMPLE: *These mice move by hopping.*
>
> *These **little grey** rodents have **long**, rather **stupid-looking** faces, **big semi-transparent** ears shaped like a mule's, and **long hind** legs on which they at times hop like **miniature** kangaroos.*

Rewrite each sentence using descriptive adjectives for each of the nouns in italics.

1. Instantly the *owl* pounced on the *snake*.

   _____

2. The *dog* waddled across the *street*.

   _____

3. Leaving the *bike* in the *ditch*, she started to cross the *field*.

   _____

   _____

4. The *man* in the *overalls* was smoking a *cigar*.

   _____

5. Moving silently through the *grass*, the *tiger* crept toward the *antelope*.

   _____

   _____

6. At the corner the *woman* turned and disappeared into a *building*.

   _____

   _____

7. Suddenly a *flash* of lightning filled the *sky*.

   _____

8. Half an hour later the *stranger* reached the *cabin*.

   _____

Exercise 65 (Sentence Construction)

Choosing Adjectives Carefully

Did you know that English contains more words than any other language? There are at least 600 000 English words. Because many of these words are adjectives, you should choose your descriptive words very carefully. Try not to use overworked adjectives such as *nice*, *awful*, *cute*, and *interesting*. Instead of always using a general word such as *big*, try substituting specific words such as *enormous*, *monstrous*, or *gigantic*.

Write at least three adjectives that could be used to describe each of these topics. Take time to choose carefully. In each group of adjectives that you choose, circle the one that you think is the most descriptive.

EXAMPLE: A climber after reaching the top of Mount Everest

excited, happy, delighted, exhausted, tired
_____

1. A diver as a shark approaches

   _____

   _____

   _____

2. Your mother if she won ten million dollars in a lottery

   _____

   _____

3. Young children at a birthday party

   _____

4. A baseball coach before an important game

   _____

5. A long-distance runner at the end of a difficult cross-country race

   _____

6. A hiker lost on a mountain as night comes and the temperature drops below zero

   _____

UNIT
18

Editing to Eliminate Unnecessary Words

When you edit your written work, take time to see whether you have used more words than necessary. Good writers always try to say what they have to say in as few words as possible. Here are some guidelines to help you.

1. Often two or more sentences can be combined to make one sentence.

   EXAMPLE: Vancouver has an unusual clock. This clock is run by steam. It is the only one of its kind in the world.
   Vancouver's unusual steam clock is the only one of its kind in the world.

2. Leave out words that duplicate information that is already in the sentence.

   EXAMPLE: In my opinion I think we should leave at 9:00 a.m. in the morning.
   An elephant is very large in size.

   Which words could be left out of those sentences?

3. Do not use two adjectives that are synonyms to describe the same noun.

   *EXAMPLE: That house has been **empty** and **vacant** since last March.*

Each of these sentences has unnecessary words. Rewrite each sentence, leaving out as many words as you can without changing the meaning.

1. My new mountain bike is bright red in colour.

   _____

2. In my opinion I think that Kaitlyn is the best goalie.

   _____

3. In the year 1608 Champlain sailed by ship up the St. Lawrence River.

   _____

4. The Grey Cup game is an annual event that takes place every year.

   _____

5. During our summer vacation last summer we visited a fascinating museum. It is called the Costume Museum of Canada. It is in Winnipeg.

   _____

   _____

A. Punctuate the following sentences correctly.

1. I've never seen them before insisted Eric

2. How do you know this demanded Officer Chen

3. I thought about going replied Becky but I've decided not to

4. Stay away from that window shouted the detective

5. Would you like me to get you a drink asked the nurse

6. If you're going to Bonavista said Jake could I please have a ride

7. Pardeep paused briefly and then asked are you feeling all right

8. Make it fast whatever you do urged Marissa

B. Cross out the incorrect verb in each of the following sentences.

1. There (is, are) almost three minutes left.

2. Neither Jose nor Samuel (has, have) finished the race.

3. On Sundays there (is, are) fewer buses.

4. Either Wendy or Gretchen (is, are) always there.

5. (Has, Have) the players from Aldergrove arrived yet?

6. (Do, Does) either Matthew or his brother play for the Wildcats?

7. (Isn't, Aren't) there any pamphlets on reptiles in the filing cabinet?

8. Both the cat and the dog (needs, need) to be fed.

9. Usually Marissa or Marco (unlock, unlocks) the door.

C. Edit each of the following sentences by crossing out the unnecessary words.

1. My brother was very extremely excited to win a lesson on sky-diving with a parachute.

2. In my opinion I think that our school should have a girls' soccer team.

3. My cousins drove by car to Parry Sound yesterday and arrived at about midnight.

4. The thunderstorm began at 3:30 p.m. in the afternoon.

Review (continued)

D. Five of the following sentences contain an error. Cross out the incorrect word and write your correction directly above it. Put a check mark in front of the two correct sentences.

1. I would advice you not to go.

2. My father works every day except Thursday.

3. We were already to leave for Aklavik when we heard the news.

4. Our family will be altogether in Joliette in March.

5. Where did you put the wash clothes?

6. What did your teacher advise you to do?

7. Everyone accept my brother went home.

E. Change each pair of sentences into one good sentence with a compound subject or a compound predicate. Leave out any words that are unnecessary. In some sentences you will have to change the verb.

1. The security officers opened the bags. The security officers checked the passengers' passports.

2. My father is flying to Yellowknife on Flight 104. My grandfather is flying to Yellowknife on the same flight.

3. The bookstore is on level three of the terminal. The lost and found office is also on level three.

4. Air traffic controllers must speak clearly over the radio. They must also think quickly.

Exercise 67 (Word Skills)
More Confusing Words

These are some words that you need to be careful with because they look or sound similar.

1.	**desert**	very dry land on which few plants grow	We used camels to cross the *desert*.
	dessert	food served at the end of a meal	Brent had ice cream for *dessert*.
2.	**loose**	not fastened firmly	Several bolts in the plane were *loose*.
	lose	to misplace, to fail to win	Did you *lose* your jacket?
3.	**quiet**	without noise	At sunrise the lake was *quiet*.
	quite	very much or completely	Are you *quite* sure you saw her?
4.	**than**	(used in comparison)	Hannah is taller *than* Kristen.
	then	at that time	Sergei will be here by *then*.
5.	**were**	past tense of are	The boys *were* disappointed.
	where	in what place	*Where* do you live?
6.	**weather**	wind, temperature, and moisture	The *weather* today is cold and windy.
	whether	if	Do you know *whether* you can go?

Eight of the following sentences contain an error. Cross out the incorrect word and write your correction directly above it. Put a check mark (✓) in front of the two correct sentences.

1. Do you know weather or not Jasmine will come?

2. Reaching the top of the cliff was quiet difficult.

3. Where did Tinisha loose the necklace?

4. You must decide whether to take the train or the plane.

5. Kelsey is faster then Natalie.

6. On Tuesday we always have apple pie for desert.

7. Suddenly the weather became quite cold.

8. A lose wheel probably caused the accident.

9. I hope she will arrive before than.

10. Were did you leave the hammer?

Exercise 68 (Composition Construction)

Writing Conversations

One way to make the characters in your stories come alive is to have them talk directly to each other. When you use conversation, however, be sure to punctuate correctly. Here are two punctuation rules to keep in mind.

1. Start a new paragraph each time the speaker changes.
2. If a quotation is made up of several sentences, put one set of quotation marks at the beginning of the first sentence. The second set goes at the end of the last sentence.

You can make conversations more appealing by using words other than *said* to tell exactly how people feel as they speak.

A. Rewrite the following conversation using direct quotations. Remember to begin a new paragraph each the time the speaker changes.

Shannon asked her father whether she could go skateboarding with Melissa. Her father said she could go if she had finished all her homework and promised to be home by nine o'clock. As Shannon raced out the door, she told her father that she had completed her homework at school and that she and Melissa would be skateboarding at Cottonwood Park. Her father called after her to remind her to wear her helmet and knee pads.

_____

_____

_____

_____

_____

_____

_____

_____

_____

B. The following story could be told in a much more exciting way by using conversation.

On their way back from a hike Luke and Tejinder noticed fresh bear tracks. Both boys had attended a program where a naturalist explained what to do while hiking in bear country. Tejinder suggested that they make lots of noise to let the bear know they were in the area. Luke looked worried and said he wished they were back at the campground. Suddenly the boys heard a branch snap. Luke said he was afraid. The boys saw a large bear walking toward them. Luke suggested they climb a tree. Tejinder said that they didn't have time. He reminded Luke that grizzlies can run more than fifty kilometres an hour. When the bear was just sixty metres from the boys, it suddenly stopped, stood on its hind legs, and sniffed the air. Suddenly the huge animal gave a loud "woof," dropped to all fours, and crashed into the underbrush. Luke said they should get out of there quickly. Tejinder agreed, but said not to run because bears will chase fast-moving objects. He told Luke to remember that you'll never win a race with a bear.

_____

_____

_____

_____

_____

_____

_____

_____

_____

_____

_____

_____

_____

UNIT
19

Exercise 69 (Punctuation and Capitalization)

Quotation Marks with Titles

Quotation marks are used around the titles of short stories, poems, songs, chapters in a book, and articles in a magazine or newspaper.

> EXAMPLE: *The only song my little sister knows is "Pop Goes the Weasel."*
>
> *"A Day in the Life of a Garbologist" is the title of the article on page 52.*

When a title is part of a quotation, put single quotation marks around the title.

> EXAMPLE: *"Can you play 'Three Blind Mice' on the piano?" asked Courtney.*

Be particularly careful when the title comes at the end of the quotation.

> EXAMPLE: *"Can you play 'Three Blind Mice'?" asked Courtney.*

Remember that all the important words in a title should have capitals. *A, an, the, of,* and *and* are capitalized only when they are the first word in the title.

Punctuate each of the following sentences correctly and circle letters that should be upper case.

1. the poem I enjoyed most was why nobody pets the lion at the zoo

2. colby played a song called blue danube waltz on the violin at the school concert

3. be sure to read chapter four exploring the northwest before tuesday said ms tomkins

4. at the end of the party everyone sang happy birthday

5. the poem the owl and the pussycat by edward lear is one of my favourites

6. the last chapter in the book is called safe at last

7. did you read the article tigers lose third straight in the paper last night asked maria

8. we drew a series of pictures to illustrate the poem the tale of custard the dragon by ogden nash

9. the program began when the band marched into the stadium playing march of the emperors

10. the title of chapter eleven replied erin is poisonous snakes of brazil

Exercise 70 (Word Skills)

Words with Suffixes

A **suffix** is a word part added to the end of a root word to form a new word.

EXAMPLE: *home + less = homeless   cheer + ful = cheerful*

Sometimes words have two suffixes.

EXAMPLE: *hope + less + ly = hopelessly   thought + ful + ness = thoughtfulness*

A. Each of these groups has a root, a prefix, and a suffix. Decide which is the prefix, which is the root, and which is the suffix. Use the three parts to form a word.

EXAMPLE: cork ed un _uncorked_

   1. month tri ly

      _____

   2. able forget un

      _____

   3. trust dis ful

      _____

   4. mis ing understand

      _____

   5. ly correct in

      _____

   6. continent al trans

      _____

   7. pre ing pay

      _____

   8. pack re ed

      _____

   9. un able beat

      _____

  10. ly semi annual

      _____

B. Using each of these words as a root, write a new word that has two suffixes. Use your dictionary if necessary.

   1. help _____

   2. joy _____

   3. danger _____

   4. fear _____

   5. sleep _____

   6. cheer _____

   7. care _____

   8. fool _____

   9. skill _____

  10. dream _____

  11. force _____

  12. hope _____

UNIT
20

Exercise 71 (Grammar and Usage)

Using Adverbs with Verbs

Adverbs do for verbs what adjectives do for nouns. An adverb adds to the meaning of a verb. Its job is to explain *when, where, how,* or *how often* something happened.

> EXAMPLE: *The plane from Grande Prairie arrived **early**.*

The adverb *early* tells *when* the plane arrived.

> EXAMPLE: *Andrew searched **everywhere** for the missing key.*

The adverb *everywhere* tells *where* Andrew searched.

> EXAMPLE: *The snake slid **slowly** toward the trapped mouse.*

The adverb *slowly* tells *how* the snake slid.

> EXAMPLE: *My father drives his truck to Charlottetown **daily**.*

The adverb *daily* tells *how often* he drives to Charlottetown.

Circle all the verbs in the following sentences. Some sentences have more than one verb. Then underline the single-word adverbs. Above each adverb write whether it tells *where, when,* or *how.* The number in parentheses tells you how many adverbs are in each sentence.

                 how

EXAMPLE: Jeremy skillfully steered the shopping cart. (1)

1. We waited patiently for the light to change. (1)

2. The two girls immediately ran indoors. (2)

3. "Don't be silly!" replied Zev angrily. (1)

4. My parents give me my allowance weekly. (1)

5. Suddenly the man darted quickly into the old barn. (2)

6. Eventually the sun shone brightly. (2)

7. Mr. Petrovich straightened his tie nervously and then stepped outside. (3)

8. The detective approached the stranger cautiously. (1)

9. I watched helplessly as the strange creature slid slowly forward. (3)

10. We searched everywhere for Jessica's hamster. (1)

Exercise 72 (Sentence Construction)

Adverbs Make the Meaning Clear

You can use adverbs to make the meaning of the verbs in your sentences more precise and more exciting.

In the following sentences the verbs are printed in boldface type. Rewrite each sentence and add imaginative adverbs to explain *how, when,* or *where* the action took place. Use a different adverb in each sentence.

EXAMPLE: Several strange creatures **jumped** from the flying saucer.

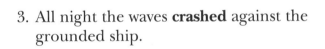

Several strange creatures jumped clumsily from the flying saucer.

1. The enormous snake **slithered** through the dense jungle.

   _____

   _____

2. The astronomer **peered** through her telescope at the new galaxy.

   _____

   _____

   _____

3. All night the waves **crashed** against the grounded ship.

   _____

   _____

   _____

4. The dazed boxer **stumbled** across the ring.

   _____

   _____

5. The skier **swerved** to the left and crashed into the tree.

   _____

   _____

UNIT 20

Turning Adjectives into Adverbs

Most adjectives can be made into adverbs by adding the suffix -*ly*.

> EXAMPLE: *A **quiet** walk*   *The woman walked **quietly**.*
> *A **sudden** stop*   *The car stopped **suddenly**.*

Not all words that end in -*ly* are adverbs. A few adjectives also end in -*ly*.

> EXAMPLE: *friendly (the friendly dog), lonely (a lonely beach),*
> *lovely (a lovely sunset)*

In addition, a few common adverbs do not end in -*ly*.

> EXAMPLE: *seldom, often, here, there, everywhere*

Circle the verb and underline the adverbs in each of the following sentences. Remember that adverbs tell *when, where,* or *how* something happened. Pay close attention to words that end in -*ly*. You should find twenty-five adverbs.

1. Instantly the detective threw the strange box outside.

2. Open the door slowly and carefully.

3. The curious opossum cautiously moved back.

4. John and his sister frequently arrive early.

5. Brett usually comes here after school.

6. The lively puppy barked constantly.

7. Yesterday Ms. Sutton searched everywhere for the missing tarantula.

8. Suddenly the deadly snake darted forward.

9. The kitten then tugged playfully at my jacket.

10. A shadowy form raced quickly across the road.

11. Soon the snow completely blocked the narrow trail.

12. The moon shone brightly on the lonely street.

13. After Tyler's speech, the crowd quickly moved outside.

14. The fire started downstairs in the family room.

15. Without waiting for an answer, Marty impatiently left the room.

Let's review what you have learned about adverbs.

1. An adverb is a word that tells *when*, *where*, *how*, or *how often*.

2. Adverbs often end with the suffix *-ly*.

A third way to find out whether a word is an adverb is to try shifting it to a different spot in the sentence. Most adverbs can be moved from one place to another without changing the meaning of the sentence. Notice, for example, how easily the adverb *frequently* changes position in these sentences.

EXAMPLE: **Frequently** *Andrew played quarterback.*
Andrew **frequently** *played quarterback.*
Andrew played quarterback **frequently**.

A. Using the clues, circle all eleven adverbs in the following sentences.

1. The friendly dog came immediately when Rachel whistled.

2. Danielle eagerly opened the small package.

3. Carefully Yazeen moved the handle backwards.

4. The lonely child walked slowly homeward.

5. Then Cody angrily slammed the door.

6. Wash the sweater properly or it will shrink.

7. Yesterday the rain fell continuously.

B. Find the adverb in each sentence. Then rewrite each sentence, moving the adverb to a different position.

1. Jason eagerly played video games whenever he got the chance.

    _____

2. Cautiously the astronaut stepped outside the space module.

    _____

3. The clown juggled six flaming torches expertly.

    _____

4. Tinisha asked timidly for directions.

    _____

Exercise 75 (Sentence Construction)

Using Verbs and Adverbs Effectively

Remember that adverbs add a more specific meaning to verbs by providing information on *when*, *where*, *how*, or *how often* the action of the verb took place.

Write sentences telling about each of these situations. Be sure to use action-packed verbs to help the reader imagine exactly what happened. In each sentence use at least one lively adverb to make the meaning of the verb clearer. Circle the adverbs in your sentences.

EXAMPLE: a shark attacking a group of smaller fish

Instantly the enormous shark whirled and slashed savagely through the school of smaller fish.

1. two racing cars colliding on a corner

_____

_____

2. children leaving school for the summer

_____

_____

_____

3. a weight-lifter struggling with a heavy lift

_____

_____

_____

4. an elephant charging a Jeep full of tourists

_____

_____

5. a puppy in an animal shelter who has just been adopted

_____

_____

Exercise 76 (Grammar and Usage)
Problems with *Good* and *Well*

Two words that are often used incorrectly are *well* and *good*.
   Well is used as an adverb to tell how something is done.

   EXAMPLE: *Olivia learned to dive* **well** *at camp.*

   Well may also be used as an adjective to mean "in good health."

   EXAMPLE: *On Tuesday Nicholas had a headache and didn't feel* **well**.

   Good is always an adjective and should never be used as an adverb.

   EXAMPLE: *Yesterday was a* **good** *day for skiing.*

A. Fill in each blank with *good* or *well*.

   1. Did you have a _____ time at the school picnic Friday?

   2. Because Laura didn't study, she didn't do _____ on her science test.

   3. Twenty out of fifty on a math test is not a _____ mark.

   4. Although I practise the piano every day, I still don't play very _____.

B. Write an answer to each of these questions. Use *well* or *good* in each answer.

   1. How did you sleep last night?

   _____

   2. How do Mrs. Hillmer's pies taste?

   _____

   3. How did the radio work after you fixed it?

   _____

   4. How did Megan feel after eating ten pancakes?

   _____

C. In your notebook write three sentences of your own. In the first sentence use *good* as an adjective. In the second sentence use *well* as an adverb. In the third sentence use *well* as an adjective.

Exercise 77 (Word Skills)

Suffixes and Spelling: Part 1

You have probably noticed that the spelling of some root words changes when suffixes are added. Sometimes it is difficult to recognize the original root word.

EXAMPLE: mischief – mischievous   destroy – destructive

Learning the following rules will improve your spelling.
1. Words that end in a silent e usually keep the e before adding a suffix beginning with a consonant.

EXAMPLE: hope + ful = hopeful   measure + ment = measurement

Four exceptions to this rule are   argue + ment = argument
            whole + ly = wholly   true + ly = truly   nine + th = ninth
2. Words that end in a silent e usually drop the e before adding a suffix beginning with a vowel.

EXAMPLE: trade + ing = trading   excite + able = excitable
            adventure + ous = adventurous

Two exceptions to this rule are
            acre + age = acreage and notice + able = noticeable
Words such as *die*, *lie*, and *tie* change the *ie* to *y* before adding *-ing*.

EXAMPLE: die + ing = dying   lie + ing = lying   tie + ing = tying

3. Words that end in ce or ge usually drop the e before adding a suffix that begins with e, *i*, or *y*.

EXAMPLE: spice + y = spicy   large + er = larger   produce + ing = producing

Words that end in ce or ge usually keep the e before a suffix that begins with any letter other than e, *i*, or *y*.
    EXAMPLE: nice + ly = nicely   large + ness = largeness

Using these rules, write the word that is formed when the following root words and suffixes are joined.

1. safe + ly = _____

2. ice + y = _____

3. excite + ment = _____

4. move + able = _____

5. circle + ing = _____

6. polite + ness = _____

7. untie + ing = _____

8. true + ly = _____

9. advertise + ment = _____

10. notice + able = _____

Exercise 78 (Word Skills)

Suffixes and Spelling: Part 2

Here are some rules for adding suffixes to words that end in *y*.

1. Words ending in *y* preceded by a consonant usually change the *y* to *i* before any suffix except one beginning with *i*.

   EXAMPLE: *try + ed = tried*   but   *try + ing = trying*
              rely + able = reliable   but   *rely + ing = relying*

In English a few one-syllable words end in a consonant and the letter *y*. Dictionaries often give two spellings for these words when suffixes are added.

   EXAMPLE: *fly + er (a person who flies or an advertisement on one sheet of paper) may be spelled* **flyer** *or* **flier**

2. Words ending in *y* preceded by a vowel usually keep the *y* when a suffix is added.

   EXAMPLE: *enjoy + able = enjoyable*   *pray + ed = prayed*
              destroy + ing = destroying

Three exceptions to this rule are
            day + ly = daily   *say + ed = said*   *lay + ed = laid*

Join these word parts to make new words.

1. joy + ful = _____

2. magnify + ed = _____

3. multiply + ing = _____

4. greedy + ness = _____

5. repay + ed = _____

6. leafy + est = _____

7. easy + er = _____

8. disobey + ed = _____

9. supply + ing = _____

10. creepy + est = _____

11. sleepy + ness = _____

12. reply + ed = _____

13. play + ed = _____

14. fly + ing = _____

15. annoy + ed = _____

16. shy + est = _____

17. worry + ed = _____

18. happy + ness = _____

Exercise 79 (Punctuation and Capitalization)

The Apostrophe with Contractions

A **contraction** is two words shortened into one. The word contraction comes from the word *contract* meaning "to shrink," or "to make smaller."

EXAMPLE: *he + will = he'll*   *they + have = they've*

Notice that an apostrophe takes the place of the missing letter or letters.
Often contractions are used to join a verb with the word *not*. Usually you simply shorten *not* to *n't* and join it to the verb.

EXAMPLE: *should + not = shouldn't*   *do + not = don't*
        were + not = weren't   *are + not = aren't*

Two exceptions to this rule are
        can + not (or cannot) = can't   *will + not = won't*
Contractions are also used to join a pronoun with forms of the verbs *be*, *have*, *will*, and *would*. In these contractions replace the first letter or letters of the verb with an apostrophe.

EXAMPLE : *they + are = they're*   *I + will = I'll*
        she + had = she'd   *we + would = we'd*

Rewrite each of the following sentences. Use contractions wherever you can.

1. I am sure you would enjoy the concert.

   _____

2. Will she not be in Ottawa?

   _____

3. You have said that before.

   _____

4. I have almost finished my spelling.

   _____

5. She would prefer that we were not there.

   _____

6. They would like to come on Thursday.

   _____

Exercise 80 (Punctuation and Capitalization)

The Apostrophe with Possessives

Nouns that show who or what something belongs to are called **possessive nouns**.

> EXAMPLE: the bracelet belonging to Amy   **Amy's** bracelet
> the wheel belonging to the tractor   the **tractor's** wheel

Here are the rules for using an apostrophe to show ownership, or possession.
1. With singular nouns add an apostrophe followed by an *s*.

> EXAMPLE: **Michael's** brother won first prize in pole vaulting.

Be careful when you add *'s* to singular nouns ending with more than one *s* sound. The word that is formed is difficult to say because it has too many *s* sounds.

> EXAMPLE: The **princess's** orders were quickly obeyed.

With such words you can form the possessive by simply adding an apostrophe.

> EXAMPLE: The **princess'** orders were quickly obeyed.

2. With plural nouns ending in *s*, add only an apostrophe.

> EXAMPLE: The **horses'** harnesses need repairing. (The harnesses belonging to the horses.)

3. With plural nouns ending with a letter other than *s*, add an apostrophe and *s*.

> EXAMPLE: The **men's** feet were badly swollen.

4. When something is owned jointly by two or more people, make only the final noun possessive.

> EXAMPLE: **Kathy and Marika's** science project fell in the pool.

Rewrite each group of words using apostrophes.

1. the fender of the car _____

2. the relatives of Mr. Timnus _____

3. the coats belonging to the ladies _____

4. the tent belonging to Ashley and Sophia _____

5. the footprints of the astronauts _____

Exercise 81 (Paragraph Construction)

Writing Descriptive Paragraphs

The place where a story happens is called the **setting**. When you write a paragraph describing a setting, you must create a picture for the reader. Unlike an artist who can use paint, brushes, and paper, a writer must rely only on words. Try to make your writing so accurate and complete that an artist could paint the scene from your description.

Here are some suggestions that will help you write good descriptions.

1. Decide what general feeling, or impression, you want the reader to have about the place you are describing. That general feeling is called a main idea.

2. Once you have decided on the main idea, choose some details that will help the reader see and feel what you have in mind.

3. Now look over the list of details. Arrange them in the best order.

4. When you write the paragraph, put the main idea in the topic sentence. All the other sentences must explain the topic sentence in some way.

A. In the following paragraph the author uses a cabin as a setting. Read the description carefully. Then answer the questions.

Once inside I quickly realized that the cabin had been deserted for years. Torn, mouldy curtains flapped gently in the breeze from many broken windows. Pieces of glass and dozens of tin cans littered the floor. Only the rusted springs of the mattress remained. For years, generations of mice had used the stuffing to line their nests. A porcupine, apparently the cabin's latest owner, peered at me intently from a pile of rotten firewood.

1. What was the writer's general impression of the cabin?

   _____

2. Which word in the topic sentence tells the main idea? _____

3. List five details the author uses to support the main idea.

   _____

   _____

   _____

   _____

   _____

Writing Descriptive Paragraphs (continued)

B. Suppose you were writing a story about an adventure on an imaginary planet called Wantuk. The spacecraft carrying your hero to Wantuk has just landed. As the door opens, she gets her first glimpse of the surface of Wantuk. Close your eyes and try to see the planet in your mind. What general impression of Wantuk do you want the reader to have? Think of an adjective that would describe the whole scene. You might decide to make Wantuk appear colourful, unusual, attractive, or frightening. Write the adjective you select in the blank in the following topic sentence.

As the door slowly slid open, Denise got her first view of the
_____ landscape of Wantuk.

The next step is to think of six to ten details that illustrate the main idea in your topic sentence.

1. _____

2. _____

3. _____

4. _____

5. _____

6. _____

7. _____

8. _____

9. _____

10. _____

C. Now, using the topic sentence and the details you have listed, write a paragraph describing Wantuk. Use specific details and imaginative nouns, verbs, adjectives, and adverbs to make your description as vivid as possible.

_____

_____

_____

_____

_____

_____

_____

_____

_____

_____

_____

_____

_____

_____

_____

_____

_____

_____

_____

_____

_____

Exercise 82 (Word Skills)

Suffixes and Spelling: Part 3

Here are some rules for adding suffixes to words ending in a single consonant.

One-syllable words ending in a consonant following a single vowel usually double the consonant before a suffix that begins with a vowel.

EXAMPLE: *drum + er = drummer   flat + est = flattest   tap + ing = tapping*

The final consonant in one-syllable words is not doubled if
1. the word ends in *x*

EXAMPLE: *wax + ed = waxed   fix + ing = fixing*

2. the suffix begins with a consonant

EXAMPLE: *tub + ful = tubful   sad + ness = sadness   glad + ly = gladly*

3. there are two vowels before the final consonant

EXAMPLE: *squeak + ed = squeaked   boil + ing = boiling   load + er = loader*

4. the word ends in more than one consonant

EXAMPLE: *brush + ed = brushed   spark + ing = sparking   truck + er = trucker*

Join these word parts to make new words.

1. slip + ing = _____
2. hard + est = _____
3. six + th = _____
4. brag + ed = _____
5. jail + er = _____
6. hat + less = _____
7. heat + ing = _____
8. jog + er = _____
9. short + est = _____
10. clean + er = _____
11. red + ish = _____
12. start + ed = _____

13. wet + ing = _____
14. mix + ed = _____
15. trip + ed = _____
16. out + er = _____

Exercise 83 (Grammar and Usage)
Making Comparisons

When you point out how things are alike or how they are different, you are making **comparisons**. Most adjectives and adverbs have different forms to show comparison. If you compare *two* persons, animals, places, or things, use the **comparative** form.

EXAMPLE: *The Atlantic Ocean is* **larger** *than the Indian Ocean.*

If you compare *three or more* items, always use the **superlative** form.

EXAMPLE: *The Pacific Ocean is the* **largest** *in the world.*

Most one-syllable adjectives and adverbs use -*er* and -*est* in comparisons.

		Comparative Form	Superlative Form
Adjective	new	newer	newest
Adverb	soon	sooner	soonest

Most adjectives and adverbs of two or more syllables use *more* and *most* in comparisons.

		Comparative Form	Superlative Form
Adjective	difficult	more difficult	most difficult
Adverb	carelessly	more carelessly	most carelessly

A. Write the comparative and superlative forms of the following adjectives and adverbs.

	Comparative	Superlative
1. old	_____	_____
2. honest	_____	_____
3. green	_____	_____
4. loud	_____	_____
5. necessary	_____	_____
6. speedy	_____	_____
7. difficult	_____	_____
8. fabulous	_____	_____
9. silly	_____	_____
10. hot	_____	_____

Making Comparisons (continued)

B. In each sentence circle the correct form of the adjective or adverb. On the line below each sentence explain the reason for your choice.

1. Dylan is the (older, oldest) player on the softball team.

   _____

2. Which of the two rivers is the (longer, longest) one?

   _____

3. Mount Logan in the Yukon is the (higher, highest) mountain in Canada.

   _____

4. This problem is (more difficult, most difficult) than the one at the top of the page.

   _____

5. In this area February is usually the (wetter, wettest) month of the year.

   _____

6. Who swam (farther, farthest), James, Rory, or Miguel?

   _____

7. The (taller, tallest) of the three trees is a hemlock.

   _____

8. Molly is the (more intelligent, most intelligent) student in class.

   _____

9. Which of the three movies did you think was the (most exciting, more exciting) one?

   _____

10. The clipper ship Cutty Sark had one of the (shorter, shortest) times for the trip from India to Europe.

    _____

11. Other than human beings, the (more intelligent, most intelligent) animals are apes.

    _____

Exercise 84 (Grammar and Usage)
Comparing Irregular Adjectives and Adverbs

The word **irregular** means "not regular," or "not according to the rules." In English a few adjectives and adverbs form comparisons in irregular ways. Which of the following sentences sounds correct to you?

Last night's storm was **badder** than last Tuesday's.
Last night's storm was **more bad** than last Tuesday's.
Last night's storm was **worse** than last Tuesday's.

You are correct if you chose the last sentence. The comparative form of *bad* is *worse*, not *badder* or *more bad*. Here is a list of the most common irregular adjectives and adverbs.

Adjective	Comparative	Superlative
many	more	most
good	better	best
bad	worse	worst
little	less	least
much	more	most
Adverb	**Comparative**	**Superlative**
well	better	best
badly	worse	worst

Complete each sentence with either the comparative or the superlative form of the word in boldface type. Not all the adjectives in this exercise are irregular.

1. Jake took only a **little** food on the hike.

   Unfortunately Nassim had even _____.

2. That car is certainly **expensive**, but the one in the

   window is _____.

3. Although all the players on the soccer team had

   many bruises, Samantha had the _____.

4. The pizza at the Alexander Hotel is **good**, but the _____ Italian food in the city is at Lorenzo's.

5. The storm today was **bad**, but the one last Friday was _____.

6. Madison plays tennis **well**, but Inga plays _____.

Exercise 85 (Grammar and Usage)

Using *Lie* and *Lay* Correctly

Many people have trouble with the verbs *lie* and *lay*. A **direct object** is a word that tells who or what received the action of the verb.

EXAMPLE: *Emily **hit** the ball over the fence.*

In this sentence the action is hitting. What did Emily hit? The *ball* is the direct object of the verb *hit*.

1. The verb *lay* always takes a direct object.

EXAMPLE: *Ryan **laid** the book on the table. He is **laying** the book on the table.*

2. The verb *lie* never takes a direct object.

EXAMPLE: *After dinner my mother will **lie** down for a rest.*

The verb in this sentence does not have a direct object.
The verb *lie* can be confusing because the past tense is *lay*.

EXAMPLE: *Yesterday my mother **lay** down for a rest.*

Study the following chart carefully to learn the tenses of these problem verbs.

Present Tense	Present Participle	Past Tense	Past Participle
lie (*recline or rest*)	are lying	lay	have lain
lay (*put down or place*)	are laying	laid	have laid

Cross out the incorrect word in parentheses in each of the following sentences. Be prepared to explain your answers.

1. The old man (laid, lay) the ring carefully on the table.

2. Roula (lay, laid) on the floor to watch television.

3. Our dog always (lies, lays) in front of the fireplace.

4. Her clothes (were laying, were lying) all over the floor.

5. On the sidewalk (lay, laid) the missing ring.

6. Lauren likes to (lie, lay) on the grass.

7. Andrew (is lying, is laying) his guitar in its case.

Exercise 86 (Punctuation and Capitalization)

Problems with Apostrophes

Pronouns, like nouns, can be used to show possession. The five possessive pronouns below are often used incorrectly. Remember that contractions are two words shortened into one. The apostrophe shows that letters have been left out. Possessive pronouns show who something belongs to. They do *not* use an apostrophe.

Contractions	Possessive Pronouns
it's (it is)	its (its ears)
they're (they are)	their (their baggage)
there's (there is)	theirs (belonging to them)
who's (who is)	whose (whose trumpet)
you're (you are)	your (your parachute)

Circle the correct word in each of the following sentences.

1. (It's, Its) almost time for (you're, your) train to leave.

2. (They're, Their) not leaving until (you're, your) finished.

3. Do you know (who's, whose) taking (they're, their) place?

4. If (it's, its) not raining on Saturday, (they're, their) planning to climb Mount Baldy.

5. At the moment (it's, its) not clear (who's, whose) to blame.

6. (You're, Your) cat is always cleaning (it's, its) fur.

7. Have you heard (who's, whose) camera (they're, their) using?

8. (It's, Its) possible that (they're, their) car will be ready for five o'clock.

9. So (you're, your) the boy (who's, whose) bicycle was stolen.

10. Has (you're, your) coach told you (who's, whose) playing right wing?

11. (There's, Theirs) a student in our school (who's, whose) older sister won a gold medal in gymnastics at the Olympics.

12. (Your, You're) uniform is on your bed. (There's, Theirs) are still in the washing machine.

13. If (it's, its) still snowing by ten o'clock (they're, their) flight will probably be cancelled.

14. (They're, Their) never going to catch (they're, their) bus if they don't hurry.

Exercise 87 (Grammar and Usage)

Prepositions and Prepositional Phrases

As you know, a sentence is a group of words that makes sense by itself. Word groups such as *along the shore*, *with me*, and *in the black car*, are called **phrases**. A phrase is a group of words that depends on the rest of the sentence for its meaning.

Often phrases begin with a **preposition**. The word *preposition* comes from a Latin word meaning "to put before." Here is a list of some of the most common prepositions.

about	around	between	in	out	toward
above	at	beyond	into	outside	under
across	before	by	near	over	until
after	behind	down	of	past	up
against	below	during	off	since	upon
along	beneath	for	on	through	with
among	beside	from	onto	to	without

A group of words that begins with a preposition and ends with a noun or a pronoun is called a **prepositional phrase**.

EXAMPLE: ***toward** the cliff*   ***above** my head*   ***between** them*

***after** the explosion*   ***through** the seaweed*   ***near** me*

Circle the prepositions in each of the following sentences. Underline the prepositional phrase. The number in parentheses at the end of each sentence tells how many prepositional phrases are in the sentence.

1. The bus from Oakville stalled near the overpass. (2)

2. Diane worked at the restaurant until noon. (2)

3. The stranger in the blue jacket raced up the stairs and into the burning house. (3)

4. Along the shore boys with large nets hunted butterflies. (2)

5. After lunch the girls rested on the grassy bank. (2)

6. The dog crawled up the bank, across the path, and into the tall grass. (3)

7. As Christopher watched, the man in the blue overalls walked slowly toward the house. (2)

8. About eight o'clock Ms. Whitely sent Matt to look for me. (2)

9. Without a word, the officer walked over the bridge and into the hotel. (3)

Exercise 88 (Paragraph Construction)

Order in Descriptive Paragraphs

Here are several good ways to organize the details in descriptions:
- from left to right or right to left
- from bottom to top or top to bottom
- from near to far or far to near
- from inside to outside or outside to inside

A. The following paragraph is from a letter written by a prisoner. Read carefully to find out what she saw from the window of her cell.

Early the next morning I crawled wearily to the small, barred window and peered out. Directly below, steep cliffs plunged straight into the lake. I could hear the thud of driftwood as it slammed like a sledgehammer against the rocky shore far below. A strong north wind whipped the lake's surface into hundreds of whitecaps. Near the far shore a small boat tossed like a dead leaf on the rough water. Beyond the boat a sandy beach quickly disappeared into a tangled mass of blackberry vines. Further inland rose a dense forest. In the distance, towering over the scene like an all-powerful chieftain, stood Mount Frosty.

1. List in order the details the prisoner sees.

   a. _____

   b. _____

   c. _____

   d. _____

   e. _____

   f. _____

2. Which of the orders listed above was used in this paragraph?

   _____

3. The writer of this paragraph used three similes to make her ideas clearer. Tell what two things she compared in each of the similes.

   a. _____

   b. _____

   c. _____

B. Now choose one of the windows in your home. On the following lines, list what you can see from that window. Be sure to arrange the details in a sensible order.

Details

_____

_____

_____

_____

_____

_____

_____

On the following lines or on your computer, write a paragraph describing what you can see from your window. Your paragraph should use at least one imaginative comparison: simile, metaphor, or personification.

Paragraph

_____

_____

_____

_____

_____

_____

_____

_____

_____

_____

_____

Exercise 89 (Composition Construction)

Writing a Business Letter

Letters to companies or organizations are called business letters. Whenever you write, you must consider your **audience**, the people who will read your writing. Your audience for a business letter would be different than for an e-mail to a friend, and so you would use a different style. When you write a business letter, keep these points in mind.

1. Use plain paper and write neatly in ink or write it using a computer.
2. Make sure the margins are equal.
3. Be brief and to the point because companies are busy.

A business letter has six parts. Study the following example carefully.

1. **Heading** (your address and date)
2. **Inside address** (name and address of recipient)
3. **Salutation** (followed by a colon)
4. **Body** (be clear, concise, correct, complete, courteous)
5. **Closing** (line up with the date, use a comma, capitalize the first word)
6. **Signature** (sign your name clearly)

> (1) 3741 Martin Street
> Antigonish, NS   B2G 1P8
> March 23, 2003
>
> Mr. J. E. Williams
> Program Director
> Camp Williwaw   (2)
> Box 793
> Bertrand, NB   E0B 1J0
>
> Dear Mr. Williams: (3)
>
>   Last July one of my friends, Mark Wilby, spent three weeks at Camp Williwaw. He really enjoyed his stay and suggested that I write to see what activities you had planned for this summer.
>   I am twelve years old and very interested in both sports and photography. For the past two years I (4) have played on our school's soccer and baseball teams. I have also belonged to the Trojan Swim Team since I was eight. Last year I joined the Photography Club at Brooksview Elementary School and learned to use a camera.
>   Would you please send me some information on the program planned for Camp Williwaw for August? I am especially interested in your baseball school and the summer photography course.
>
>   Thank you very much for your help.
>   Yours truly,   (5)
>   Jeremy Collins   (6)

Writing a Business Letter (continued)

Using the sample letter on the opposite page as a model, write a letter to the director of a summer camp asking about the program. In your letter, talk about your background and some of your interests.

_____

_____

_____

_____

_____

_____

_____

_____

_____

_____

_____

_____

_____

_____

_____

_____

_____

Exercise 90 (Composition Construction)

Writing a Letter of Opinion

Here are two sentences about dogs.

Dogs have a keen sense of smell.

Dogs are more fun than cats.

The first sentence states a **fact**. Scientists who study dogs can find out exactly how well dogs can smell. The second sentence is an **opinion**. An opinion is a personal feeling about something.

Most newspapers have a section for letters from their readers. Sometimes readers comment on a story that appeared in an earlier edition. At other times people may be pointing out a situation in the community that needs improving. When you write a letter to the editor, start by clearly stating your opinion. Then present facts that support your opinion. Use a business letter format.

Here is an example of the body section of an opinion letter.

I am a grade six student at Crescent Park School in Summerside and I feel that a push-button traffic light on Pine Street in front of my school is badly needed. We have only a "Children Crossing" sign on either side of the street. I took a survey at our school and found that 187 students at Crescent Park School have to cross Pine Street each day to get to and from school. The speed limit in front of the school is thirty kilometres an hour, but many cars travel much faster.

There have already been two accidents in front of the school this year. I think it is important to do something about this situation immediately, before someone is seriously hurt.

A. In the blank at the end of each sentence write *fact* or *opinion*. Be prepared to explain your answers.

1. Winter is the best season of the year. _____

2. Last winter was the coldest on record in our area. _____

3. My father taught me to ski when I was six years old. _____

4. My older brother should be the goalie for his hockey team. _____

5. Pizza with onions tastes horrible. _____

B. Think of a situation in your school or community that needs improving. In your notebook or on the computer, write a letter to your principal or the editor of your local paper explaining what you think needs changing. Be sure to support your opinion with facts and reasons.

Exercise 91 (Grammar and Usage)

Using Phrases to Make Nouns More Precise

Prepositional phrases often give the reader important details.

 EXAMPLE: *A man took my wallet.*

This sentence tells only the basic facts. Now notice what happens when a prepositional phrase is used to describe the man.

 EXAMPLE: *A man **in a striped shirt** took my wallet.*
 *A man **with red curly hair** took my wallet.*

Adding a phrase makes the meaning of the noun much more precise. Because each of the phrases in boldface type tells us more about the noun *man*, they are called **adjective phrases**. Adjective phrases describe nouns in the same way that single adjectives do.

In each blank write an adjective phrase to make the meaning of the noun in boldface type more precise. Be sure your phrase starts with a preposition and ends with a noun or a pronoun.

EXAMPLE: The **wrestler** <u>in the purple trunks</u> is a former
    football player.

1. Did you know that the **girl** _____

    _____ is my sister?

2. The **skydiver** _____

    _____ landed in the potato field.

3. Try the **cake** _____

    _____. It's fantastic!

4. Within minutes we were surrounded by the enormous **insects**

    _____.

5. The large **cat** _____
    crept stealthily through the tall grass.

6. Both detectives were puzzled by the **footprints** _____

    _____.

7. In an instant the **seagull** _____
    grabbed my sandwich.

Exercise 92 (Grammar and Usage)
Using Adverb Phrases to Explain *When*, *Where*, and *How*

Prepositional phrases can be used to tell more about verbs in the same way that adverbs do.

> EXAMPLE: *The mail arrived* **before noon**.

The phrase "before noon" tells *when* the mail arrived.

> EXAMPLE: *The batter hit the ball* **toward left field**.

The phrase "toward left field" tells *where* the batter hit the ball.

> EXAMPLE: *The police car skidded around the corner* **on two wheels**.

The phrase "on two wheels" tells *how* the car skidded.

Phrases that explain *when*, *where*, or *how* something happened are called **adverb phrases**.

Fill in the blanks in the following sentences with adverb phrases. Be sure to follow the directions in parentheses.

1. The track meet will take place _____.
   (tell when)

2. In July Angie and Gillian hiked _____.
   (tell where)

3. Close the door _____. (tell how)

4. _____ (tell when) we went to the hockey game.

5. The old man walked _____ (tell how)

   _____. (tell where)

6. The sign _____ (tell where) said "Beware of the dog."

7. _____ (tell when) Mrs. Anderson fell asleep.

8. _____ (tell when) the old car finally stopped.

9. We can easily hike to the lake _____.
   (tell when)

Exercise 93 (Sentence Construction)

Combining Sentences with Prepositional Phrases

Sometimes you can combine a number of short sentences by using prepositional phrases.

> EXAMPLE: *The winning team ate seventy-two hamburgers. They attend Southlands School. The team finished eating in twelve minutes. The winning team from Southlands School ate seventy-two hamburgers in twelve minutes.*

Notice how the combined sentence is smoother, and how it avoids repeating some words.

In each group of sentences use the first sentence as a base. Change the other two sentences into prepositional phrases and combine them with the first sentence.

1. Our relatives are here.
   They are from Germany. They will be staying three weeks.

   _____

   _____

UNIT
25

2. My younger brother takes violin lessons.
   He has lessons on Tuesday afternoon. His teacher is
   Ms. Levinson.

   _____

   _____

   _____

3. Yesterday Sakina found a wristwatch.
   She found it near the gymnasium. It had a brown leather strap.

   _____

   _____

4. The detective searched the warehouse.
   She had a German shepherd dog. She was looking for the escaped prisoner.

   _____

   _____

Exercise 94 (Grammar and Usage)

Using Pronouns Correctly: Part 1

Words such as *she* and *they* are called **personal pronouns**.

> EXAMPLE: *Erica is my sister.* **She** *is in grade eight.*
> *Amy and Derek will be late.* **They** *slept in this morning.*

Notice that both of these pronouns take the place of nouns that are used as subjects of the sentence. Here is a list of the personal pronouns that can be used in the subject position.

Singular	Plural
I	we
you	you
he	they
she	they
it	they

Choosing the correct pronoun is usually quite easy when the subject is a single pronoun. For example, it's easy to see that "Me broke my wrist" is wrong.

Sometimes a pronoun is used with a noun or another pronoun to make a compound subject. When this happens, deciding which pronoun to use is more difficult. Which of these sentences sounds correct to you?

Melissa and she play on opposing hockey teams.

Melissa and her play on opposing hockey teams.

You can tell which sentence is correct by reading them without the words "Melissa and." That will show that *she*, not *her*, is the pronoun to use.

Write the correct pronoun in the blank at the right. Test each sentence by reading it without the noun and the word *and*.

1. Justin and (I, me) must leave early. _____

2. Jenna and (she, her) won a trip to Mexico. _____

3. The team from Sibley and (us, we) had dinner. _____

4. Mario and (I, me) often work together in science. _____

5. In August Etien and (them, they) are going to Sweden. _____

6. Unfortunately Kirsten and (her, she) were both injured. _____

7. His older brother and (he, him) are excellent swimmers. _____

8. Sen-Yee and (they, them) decided to walk home. _____

A. Write sentences using the possessive form of six of the following nouns.

girls   James   detectives   rocket   Ms. Andrews   shark   bird   Haley

_____

_____

_____

_____

_____

_____

B. Fill in the blanks in these sentences with *good* or *well,* or *lie* or *lay.*

1. My mother thought the school choir sang _____.

2. Last night we watched a _____ hockey game on television.

3. Our cat likes to _____ in front of the fire.

4. I can play soccer just as _____ as you can.

5. _____ the paintbrush carefully on the paper.

6. Brianna certainly is a _____ pianist.

7. Yesterday I _____ on the beach for three hours.

8. Who _____ that wet towel on my book?

C. In each blank write an adjective phrase to make the meaning of the noun in boldface type more precise. Be sure your phrase starts with a preposition and ends with a noun or a pronoun.

1. When the smoke cleared, I saw a strange **creature** _____.

2. The **helicopter** _____ landed safely at Prescott.

3. The **path** _____ is good for inline skating.

4. Gurdeep's mother owns the **shop** _____.

D. Circle all the adverbs in the following sentences. You should find fifteen adverbs.

1. Our daily paper usually arrives about eight o'clock in the morning.

2. Instantly Ryan threw the box outside.

3. Slowly and quietly the boys crept away.

4. Sometimes their dog barks loudly.

5. Was the sun shining brightly then?

6. Aunt Sue often complains about the weather.

7. Will your brother finally pass his driver's test tomorrow?

8. The chimpanzees swung easily and noisily through the trees.

E. Complete each of the following sentences with either the comparative or the superlative form of the word in boldface type.

1. Cameron plays hockey **well**, but Alex plays _____.

2. Ontario is a **large** province, but Quebec is the _____ province in Canada.

3. The clown on the trampoline was **funny,** but the clowns on the fire truck were the _____ of all.

4. All of the five Great Lakes are **big**. Which one is the _____?

5. Both Amber and Courtney are **good** goalies. Who do you think is

   _____?

6. Sven and Jessica are **tall**. Which one is _____?

F. In the blanks write the word that is formed when the following root words and suffixes are joined.

1. complete + ly = _____   5. dim + er = _____

2. fame + ous = _____   6. taste + less = _____

3. shy + est + _____   7. carry + ing = _____

4. announce + ment = _____   8. stir + ed = _____

Exercise 95 (Grammar and Usage)

Using Pronouns Correctly: Part 2

In Exercise 94 you studied the personal pronouns that are used in the subject position.

Sometimes personal pronouns follow an action verb. When this happens you must use an **object pronoun**.

Subject Pronouns	Object Pronouns
I kicked the ball.	The horse kicked **me**.
He dislikes Lindsey.	Lindsey dislikes **him**.
She told Jerry.	Jerry told **her**.
They invited the girls.	The girls invited **them**.
We telephoned Erin.	Erin telephoned **us**.
You followed Derek.	Derek followed **you**.
It hit the car.	The car hit **it**.

Notice that two of the pronouns, *you* and *it*, do not change form.

Sometimes an action verb is followed by a noun and a pronoun. As with subject pronouns, your ear will usually tell you when to use an object pronoun. Remember to test the sentence by reading it without the noun and the word *and*.

> EXAMPLE: *Mr. Lam took Mary and (I, me) to the basketball game.*
> *Mr. Lam took (I, me) to the basketball game.*
> *Mr. Lam took **me** to the basketball game.*

UNIT
26

In each of the following sentences choose the correct pronoun and write it in the blank. Test each sentence by reading it without the noun and the word *and*.

1. The car just missed Chessa and (we, us). _____

2. Mr. Sahota invited Evan and (I, me) to come. _____

3. Yesterday the police asked Marcus and (they, them) some questions. _____

4. My uncle took Noah and (she, her) to Spring Lake. _____

5. My parents met Jolene and (him, he) on Oak Street. _____

6. Last week Ms. Tanaka paid my sister and (I, me) thirty dollars for gardening work. _____

7. Mr. Wallansky lent Liam and (them, they) his car. _____

Exercise 96 (Word Skills)

Our Latin and Greek Roots

You probably think of television as a modern invention. Actually the word *television* was first used by scientists in 1876. They were convinced that if sound could be sent by telephone, pictures could be transmitted through the air. The parts of the word *television* are much older. They were used by the people who lived in ancient Greece and Rome. The Romans spoke a language called Latin. The Latin word *videre* means "to see." The Greek prefix *tele* means "far off." So the word *television* means "to see from far off."

English has borrowed words from many languages, but more than half our words come from Greek and Latin. Because so many English words come from these languages, learning a few important Latin and Greek roots can help you to unlock the meaning of hundreds of English words. The following chart contains the roots that are most often used.

Root	Meaning	Example	Root	Meaning	Example
annus	year	anniversary	*dynamis*	power	dynamic
aqua	water	aquarium	*geo*	earth	geography
astro	star	astronaut	*graph*	write	biography
aud	hear	audience	*mare*	sea	marine
auto	self	autograph	*meter*	measure	thermometer
bio	life	biology	*ped*	foot	pedestrian
centum	hundred	century	*script*	write	inscription
cycl	circle	bicycle	*tele*	distant	telegraph
dent	tooth	dentist	*thermo*	heat	thermostat

A. In the following list, circle the part of the word based on the Latin or Greek root, and then write a sentence using the word correctly. A word might contain more than one root. You may need to use your dictionary.

1. astronomer

   _____

2. thermos

   _____

3. autobiography

   _____

4. pedal

   _____

B. The following word search contains several words that have the Latin and Greek roots listed on the opposite page. You can find the hidden words by reading down or across. Some are written forward, but others are written backward. Words may overlap so that some letters are used for more than one word. Circle each word. Then write it beside its definition.

R	Q	A	S	C	R	I	B	B	L	E	T	Y	O
E	S	U	B	M	A	R	I	N	E	X	E	M	S
T	V	D	E	T	S	I	L	C	Y	C	L	O	N
E	N	I	T	N	E	D	T	H	E	C	E	N	T
M	E	T	E	L	E	G	R	A	M	E	P	O	R
O	P	O	M	D	T	G	O	L	S	N	H	R	I
R	O	R	I	I	I	E	L	A	V	T	O	T	D
A	C	I	T	A	M	O	T	U	A	E	N	S	E
B	S	U	I	M	A	L	R	N	W	N	E	A	N
A	E	M	R	E	N	P	T	N	E	N	I	T	T
S	L	U	A	T	Y	R	I	A	B	I	P	E	D

UNIT
26

a large room for concerts	_auditorium_	hard, bony material beneath the enamel of the teeth	_____
one hundredth of a dollar	_____	to write carelessly	_____
a spear with three points or teeth	_____	someone who rides a cycle	_____
operating by itself	_____	the study of the stars	_____
a boat that travels under water	_____	an instrument used to send voices by electricity	_____
an instrument that measures air pressure	_____	coming once a year	_____
a coded message sent over wires	_____	a two-legged animal	_____

Exercise 97 (Grammar and Usage)
Using Pronouns Correctly: Part 3

Object pronouns must be used to replace the noun or nouns at the end of a prepositional phrase.

EXAMPLE: *The bees swarmed around **Maria and Abigail**.*
*The bees swarmed around **them**.*

Which of the following sentences sounds correct to you?

Between you and I that movie was boring
Between you and me that movie was boring.

You are correct if you chose the second sentence. The pronoun *me* is needed because it is the object of the preposition *between*.

Be especially careful when a compound object follows the preposition. In the following sentences the pronouns are used correctly.

EXAMPLE: *The car rolled slowly toward Emma and **him**.*
*Ms. Axelson divided the pie equally between Marcus and **me**.*

Circle the preposition in each sentence. Write the correct pronoun in the blank at the right. You can test many of these sentences by reading them without the noun and the word *and*.

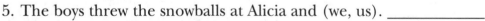

1. Divide the money between Martika and (she, her)._____

2. Are you going with Dustin and (they, them)? _____

3. I'm going to the movie with Anthony and (he, him). _____

4. Mr. Carter gave the tickets to Logan and (I, me). _____

5. The boys threw the snowballs at Alicia and (we, us). _____

6. Let's keep this a secret between you and (I, me). _____

7. The bicycles are for Anna and (she, her). _____

8. The boat left without Yasin and (he, him). _____

9. Bring some popcorn for you and (I, me). _____

Exercise 98 (Grammar and Usage)

More Practice Using Pronouns Correctly

You have learned that pronouns are used to replace nouns in three ways:

1. Subject of the sentence

   EXAMPLE: *Jenna hit a home run.* **She** *hit a home run.*

2. Following an action verb

   EXAMPLE: *We play the team from Timmins at noon. We play* **them** *at noon.*

3. Object of a preposition

   EXAMPLE: *Divide the candy between Lindsey and* **her**.

A. Some of the following sentences need subject pronouns. Others need object pronouns. Circle the correct pronoun. Test each sentence by reading it without the noun and the word *and*.

1. Are Yasin and (they, them) going skiing on Mt. Garibaldi tomorrow?

2. The team left without Nadia and (I, me).

3. The firecracker exploded near Pia and (we, us).

4. Mr. Singh told Logan and (he, him) to leave the box in the office.

5. Uncle Paul drove Vanessa and (she, her) back to Cloverdale.

6. Without warning the truck rolled toward Cassandra and (they, them).

B. Decide whether the following groups of words contain subject pronouns or object pronouns. Then write interesting sentences using them correctly.

1. Aunt Deb and him _____

   _____

2. Patrick and I _____

   _____

3. the Sternbergs and we _____

   _____

4. the seagulls and her _____

   _____

Exercise 99 (Grammar and Usage)

Using Co-ordinating Conjunctions to Join Equals

In Exercise 36 you learned that a **conjunction** is a word that joins two or more words or groups of words. The three most common conjunctions are *and*, *but*, and *or*. These words are called **co-ordinating conjunctions**. The word *co-ordinating* means "equal in importance." Co-ordinating conjunctions always join words or groups of words that are used in the same way.

> EXAMPLE: *Allen **and** David worked together to edit their story.*

The co-ordinating conjunction joins two nouns *Allen* and *David*.

> EXAMPLE : *The trail along the cliffs is breathtaking **but** dangerous.*

The co-ordinating conjunction joins two adjectives *breathtaking* and *dangerous*.

> EXAMPLE : *Leave your coats in the closet **or** on the bed.*

The co-ordinating conjunction joins two prepositional phrases, *in the closet* and *on the bed*.

A. Circle the co-ordinating conjunction in each of these sentences. Underline each of the sentence parts joined by the conjunctions. In the blank at the beginning of the sentence, tell whether the co-ordinating conjunction joined nouns, verbs, adjectives, adverbs, or prepositional phrases.

_____ 1. Amlet and Kayla will not arrive until eight o'clock.

_____ 2. The soldiers moved slowly and carefully across the field.

_____ 3. We can hike into the canyon or around Mirror Lake.

_____ 4. The weather tomorrow will be warm but wet.

_____ 5. The officer saluted and marched out the door.

B. Fill in the blanks with the part of speech noted in parentheses.

1. The ground squirrel scampered _____ but _____ into its hole. (adverbs)

2. Did Dana have _____ or _____ for dessert? (nouns)

3. The trail to Willow Falls was _____ but _____. (adjectives)

4. The boys _____ and _____ the old shed. (verbs)

Exercise 100 (Sentence Construction)

Writing Compound Sentences

Co-ordinating conjunctions can also be used to join simple sentences. A **simple sentence** has only one subject and one predicate.

> EXAMPLE: *The guards fired several warning shots.*
> *The prisoners did not stop.*

A sentence made up of two or more simple sentences is called a **compound sentence**. A comma is used before the co-ordinating conjunction.

> EXAMPLE: *The guards fired several warning shots, but the prisoners did not stop.*

When you write a compound sentence, always make sure that both parts belong together. If the simple sentences are not about the same topic, the sentences will not have unity.

Be careful not to overuse compound sentences. The compound sentence is only one of many ways to join ideas together. When you write, try to put sentences together in a variety of ways.

Write a suitable simple sentence of your own to make each of the following sentences into a compound sentence. Be sure that the sentence you add has its own subject and predicate. Remember that the two parts of the sentence must go well together.

1. On Tuesday the rescue party reached the crashed plane, but _____

   _____

2. Don't open that door, or _____

   _____

3. Suddenly the lights went out, and _____

   _____

4. The terrified mouse tried to escape, but _____

   _____

5. The stranger told us to leave immediately, or _____

   _____

6. Instantly dense smoke filled the building, and _____

   _____

Exercise 101 (Sentence Construction)

Learning to Use the Semicolon

A **semicolon** (;) looks like a comma with a period on top. Semicolons have several uses.

1. The semicolon can be used to separate the two parts of a compound sentence. When you use a semicolon, it replaces a conjunction such as *or*, *and*, or *but*. The semicolon tells the reader that the two parts of the sentence are of equal importance.

   EXAMPLE: *Lauren's cookies are good, but my grandmother's are even better.*
   Lauren's cookies are good; my grandmother's are even better.

2. Sometimes the two parts of a compound sentence are joined with connecting words or phrases such as *however, for example,* or *for this reason*. In these sentences use a semicolon after the first sentence and a comma after the connecting word or phrase.

   EXAMPLE: *A horse sleeps about three hours a day;* **on the other hand***, a koala bear sleeps for twenty-two hours each day.*

Some other connecting words that can be used in compound sentences are

consequently	for example	for instance
however	in addition	in fact
on the other hand	otherwise	therefore

Punctuate each of the following compound sentences. Do not add periods.

1. A human being's heart beats 100 800 times a day however a mouse's heart beats 720 000 times a day.

2. Elephants have very large teeth in fact the largest elephant teeth measure up to thirty centimetres long.

3. Some fish can swim very fast for example the sailfish can zip through the water at 110 kilometres an hour for short distances.

4. A cheetah can run about 113 kilometres an hour a peregrine falcon can reach speeds of 294 kilometres an hour in a dive.

5. A mouse lives for only about six years some scientists believe that the giant tortoise can live for more than one hundred years.

6. Some snakes are short in fact a thread snake may be only ten and one half centimetres long.

Exercise 102 (Composition Construction)

Report Writing: Gathering Information and Taking Notes

Suppose your teacher asked you to write a report about Iqaluit (pronounced ee-KA-loo-eet), the capital city of Nunavut.

Where would you look for information? You should certainly look in the library. Be sure to check the encyclopedia and the card catalogue for books on your topic. Magazines are also a useful source of information. Another good place to search for up-to-date material is the Internet. You could also try writing to the city of Iqaluit for information.

Once you have found some information, the next step is to take notes. First read the material through without writing anything down. Then take time to think about what you have read. Summarize the author's main ideas in your own words. It is not necessary to write complete sentences; notes can be made in point form, or sentence fragments. If you decide to quote the author exactly, be sure to put the words in quotation marks.

A good way to collect notes is to write the information on index cards. At the top of each card write the subject of the note. At the bottom of the card write the name of the author and the book or magazine where you found the information.

Underline key words and groups of words in these sentences about Iqaluit. Then use the underlined ideas to write each sentence in note form in your notebook. Use your own words wherever possible. Be sure to include all the important information.

1. Iqaluit, the largest community and the capital city of Nunavut, is located in the southeastern part of Baffin Island. Most of the people who live in Iqaluit are Inuit.

2. The name Iqaluit means "the place where the fish are" in Inuktitut, the Inuit language.

3. The average temperature in January in Iqaluit is –30°C and in July the average is 15°C. Because it is so far north, in June Iqaluit receives twenty-four hours of daylight each day, but in January the city gets just five hours of daylight.

4. According to the 2001 census, the population of Canada increased by 4 percent from 1996 to 2001. During the same time period, the population of Iqaluit increased from 4220 to 5235. This 24 percent increase made Iqaluit one of the fastest growing cities in Canada.

Exercise 103 (Composition Construction)

Report Writing: Organizing the Report

A plan for a report is called an **outline**.

> EXAMPLE: I. *Introductory paragraph*
> II. *The history of Iqaluit*
> III. *Making a living in Iqaluit*
> IV. *Interesting things to do in Iqaluit*
> V. *Concluding paragraph*

Developing an outline helps you organize your thoughts and plan the topics for your paragraphs.

A. Here are some notes from research cards on Iqaluit. Some of these ideas belong in a paragraph on the history of Iqaluit. Others should be in a paragraph about earning a living in Iqaluit. Print an **H** for history in front of each heading that belongs with that main idea. Print an **L** in front of each heading that belongs in a paragraph about earning a living.

_____ April 19, 2001, Iqaluit officially became a city

_____ In 1576 Martin Frobisher claimed Baffin Island for England

_____ World War II, U.S. Air Force built large air base here

_____ Outfitters take tourists on snowmobile and dog sled trips

_____ April 1, 1999, Iqaluit became capital of Nunavut

_____ Many people work for government

_____ Create carvings from whalebone, antler, and stone

_____ Frobisher Bay renamed Iqaluit in 1987

_____ The 2001 census finds 5235 people living in Iqaluit

_____ Rent outdoor equipment such as tents and kayaks

_____ Work in hotels and restaurants

_____ New buildings needed for government workers

B. Once you have sorted these notes into two groups, the next step is to organize the topics within each group. The cards in the history group can be organized in time, or chronological, order. Fill in the blanks in the following outline with the topics from the history cards.

The History of Iqaluit

A. From arrival of Frobisher until 1990

    1. _____

    2. _____

    3. _____

B. From 1990 to the present

    1. _____

    2. _____

    3. _____

Most people in Iqaluit work either for the government or in tourism jobs. Use this outline to organize the cards you have in the **L** group into a sensible order.

How People Earn a Living in Iqaluit

A. Government jobs

    1. _____

    2. _____

B. Looking after tourists

    1. _____

    2. _____

    3. _____

    4. _____

UNIT
28

Report Writing: The Introduction and Conclusion

When you come to write your report, start with an **introductory paragraph**. In the **body** write a series of paragraphs, each of which discusses one of your main ideas. End your report with a **concluding paragraph**.

The introductory paragraph in a report serves much the same purpose as the topic sentence in a paragraph. This paragraph must not only tell what the report will be about, but must also catch the reader's attention.

One way to do this is to begin with a question. You might try starting with "Wouldn't you like to visit a place where you can take part in igloo-building and harpoon-throwing contests?" Another possibility is to start with fascinating or surprising details.

The concluding paragraph in a report briefly summarizes the writer's ideas. Its purpose is to bring the report to a smooth ending.

Here are some details you may want to use in an opening paragraph on Iqaluit.

- Iqaluit, the smallest capital city in Canada, is the capital of Nunavut, the largest province or territory in Canada.

- On some days during the winter Iqaluit gets only four hours of sunlight. In June the city gets twenty-four hours of sunlight each day.

- Average temperatures in January and February drop to –26°C.

- There are no street addresses in Iqaluit because there are few roads. The only way to get to Iqaluit is by plane.

- Groceries are expensive in Iqaluit. Prices are two or three times higher than in southern Canada.

In your notebook, write an introductory paragraph for a report on Iqaluit.

Exercise 105 (Composition Construction)

Organizing a Bibliography

A **bibliography** is a list of the books, articles, and other sources that you used to write your report. The materials in a bibliography are listed in alphabetical order according to the authors' last names. Look carefully at the following bibliography for a report on cheetahs to learn how a bibliography is organized.

Example:

MacMillan, Dianne M., *Cheetahs*, Minneapolis: Carolrhoda Books, Inc., 1997

Schlaepfer, Gloria G., *Cheetahs*, New York: Benchmark Books, 2002

Thompson, Sharon E., *Built for Speed*, Minneapolis: Lerner Publications Company, 1998

Wielebnowski, Nadja, "Cheetah," *World Book Encyclopedia*, Volume 3, page 395, Chicago: World Book Inc., 2003

Zimmerman, Susan, "New Chance for Cheetahs," *Ranger Rick*, September 1998, Volume 32, Issue 9, page 14

Cody, Doughty, "All About Cheetahs." Retrieved Feb. 24, 2003 <http://www.expage.com/page/codydoughty>

Notice that each entry includes the author's name, the title of the work, city of publication, publisher, and date of publication. With magazine and Internet articles list the author first, followed by the title of the article in quotation marks. The titles of books and magazines go in italics, but if you are not working on a computer, underline the titles instead. For Internet sources list the URL, or Internet address, and the date you accessed that information.

Here is a list of sources for a report on Iqaluit. Using these sources, organize a bibliography for a report on Iqaluit in your notebook or on a computer.

Books
Iqaluit: Gateway to the Arctic, by Jared Keen, published by Weigl Educational Publishers Limited, in Calgary, Alberta, in 2002

Nunavut, by Lyn Hancock, published by Lerner Publications Company in Minneapolis in 1995

Magazines
A New Capital for the Arctic, by Brian Bergman, published in Maclean's on February 19, 1996, pages 20, 21

Web site
Iqaluit by Alootook Ipellie and Carol Rigby on Nunavut Handbook Home Web site, January 12, 2003, http://www.arctictravel.com/chapters/iqaluitpage.html

UNIT
29

Exercise 106 (Grammar and Usage)

Introducing Subordinating Conjunctions

When you write, you may sometimes want to join two ideas that are not equal in importance.

> EXAMPLE: *Kevin ate supper. He did his homework.*
> *Kevin ate supper **before** he did his homework.*

The first two sentences express two separate ideas. In sentence two, however, the word *before* tells us that the two ideas are related. Kevin ate supper first and then he did his homework.

The word *before* is a **subordinating conjunction**. It introduces the second idea of the sentence—"he did his homework." The words "before he did his homework" cannot stand by themselves. They become important only when you relate them to the rest of the sentence. Subordinating conjunctions introduce groups of words that depend on the main part of the sentence for their meaning.

Here are some common subordinating conjunctions.

after	because	since	unless	whenever
although	before	than	until	where
as	if	though	when	while

A. Circle the subordinating conjunctions in the following sentences. Underline the group of words that each conjunction introduces.

1. Because a rockslide blocked the trail, we could not reach the hilltop.

2. Although Jordan ran fast, he could not catch up to Antonio.

3. We cannot get home until the snowploughs clear the roads.

4. If you know the way, we'll follow you.

5. The ferry cannot sail when the wind is blowing hard.

B. Each of the following groups of words begins with a subordinating conjunction. Use each word group in a sentence of your own.

1. after Trevor broke his leg

   _____

2. when the dike broke

   _____

Exercise 107 (Grammar and Usage)
Introducing Dependent Clauses

A **clause** is a group of words that has a subject and a predicate.

   EXAMPLE: *Erin had just finished the test **when the bell rang**.*

This sentence is made up of two parts. The first part "Erin had just finished the test" is called the **main clause**, or **independent clause**. Notice that a main clause can stand alone as a sentence and make sense.

The second part of the sentence "when the bell rang" is also a clause, because it too has a subject and a predicate. This clause, however, depends on the main clause for its meaning. A clause that begins with a subordinating conjunction and depends on a main clause to make sense is called a **dependent clause**. A dependent clause cannot stand alone as a sentence.

Sometimes the independent clause comes at the end of the sentence. When this happens, use a comma to separate the dependent clause from the rest of the sentence.

   EXAMPLE: ***If we pick the blackberries,*** *Dad promised to make us a pie.*

Each sentence in this exercise has two clauses. Draw one line under the independent clause. Draw two lines under the dependent clause. Remember that dependent clauses always begin with a subordinating conjunction.

1. Unless you follow the map, you will probably get lost.

2. All the students cheered after the principal announced the holiday.

3. While we sat around the campfire, we toasted marshmallows.

4. Although it appears difficult, this trick is actually easy to do.

5. When we walked past the arena, we heard a crowd cheering.

6. Although my grandmother is sixty years old, she still enjoys playing hockey.

7. My uncle will have to sell some of his cattle unless it rains this fall.

8. As the boat pulled away from the dock, the captain blew the whistle.

9. Laura enjoys playing chess whenever she has time.

10. Although I like the shape of that skateboard, I don't like the colour.

Exercise 108 (Sentence Construction)

Using Complex Sentences

A **complex sentence** is a sentence with one independent clause and one or more dependent clauses.

              dependent clause   **independent clause**
EXAMPLE: *After the game is over, the team is planning to go to Kelly's house.*

When you write try to use a variety of simple, compound and complex sentences.

A. Some of these sentences are simple sentences. Others are compound or complex sentences. In the blank at the beginning of each sentence, identify the sentence as simple, compound, or complex. Be ready to explain your answer.

_____ 1. The moose is a large animal with a heavy body and long legs.

_____ 2. Moose hold their heads low and flatten back their ears when they are angry.

_____ 3. In summer moose often eat leafy water plants, but in winter they eat twigs and branches.

_____ 4. Sometimes moose fight off predators with their sharp hooves or antlers.

_____ 5. Moose can travel easily in snow up to seventy centimetres deep, but they often get stuck in deeper snow.

B. Combine each pair of sentences into a complex sentence. Try to use a variety of subordinating conjunctions.

1. Moose spend most of the spring, summer, and fall eating. They need fat to stay alive during the winter when food is scarce.

_____

_____

2. Sometimes moose roar like lions. They roar when they are upset.

_____

_____

Clichés: Is Your Language Worn Out?

Do you get tired of seeing the same commercial over and over on television? Perhaps you didn't realize that some similes have also been overworked. An expression that has been used too often is called a **cliché** (pronounced klē shā´).

> EXAMPLE: *as pretty as a picture   as honest as the day is long   as black as coal*

Try not to use clichés in your writing or when speaking. Instead, use original similes that compare objects in fresh and unusual ways.

Rewrite the following clichés with imaginative similes of your own.

EXAMPLE: as cold as ice   *as cold as a polar bear's nose*

1. as white as snow

   _____

2. as happy as a lark

   _____

3. as cute as a button

   _____

4. as clumsy as an ox

   _____

5. as green as grass

   _____

6. as busy as a beaver

   _____

7. as black as night

   _____

8. as gentle as a lamb

   _____

9. as hungry as a bear

   _____

UNIT
30

Exercise 110 (Sentence Construction)

More Practice with Combining Sentences

In this book you have learned five ways of joining short sentences. Review the examples in the specific exercises if you are unsure.

1. Use a compound subject or a compound predicate. (Exercise 36)
2. Turn one sentence into an appositive. (Exercise 39)
3. Change one sentence into a prepositional phrase. (Exercise 93)
4. Join two or more simple sentences to make a compound sentence. (Exercise 100)
5. Join two or more simple sentences to make a complex sentence. (Exercise 108)

The following two paragraphs from a report on grizzly bears are not well written. In your notebook or on your computer, rewrite the paragraphs making these improvements.

1. Combine sentences wherever possible. Try to use a variety of ways of joining sentences.
2. Move the subject in several of the sentences to the beginning or the end of the sentence.
3. Try not to have sentences that follow each other start with the same subject.

Grizzly bears are omnivorous. An omnivore is an animal that eats both plants and other animals. Human beings are omnivores. Grizzlies often eat vegetation, roots, berries, and insects. Some of their favourite plants are skunk cabbage and cow parsnip. They like glacier lilies and horsetail too. They also eat small rodents. Such as marmots and ground squirrels. Grizzlies rarely attack full-grown animals such as elk or deer. Unless they are sick or injured. Instead of hunting animals, they often feed on carrion. Carrion means animals that are already dead.

Grizzlies usually mate every second year. Young grizzlies are born in the den. They are born between mid-January and early March. Often a mother has twins. Sometimes she may have only one cub. Sometimes she has as many as four. At birth a bear cub weighs only half a kilogram. It is about twenty-three centimetres long. It is covered with fine hair. Young bears are born toothless. They are also blind. Their eyes do not open until they are three weeks old. The cubs stay in the den for the first three months. They grow fat on their mother's milk. Grizzly's milk is much richer than cow's milk. The cubs leave the den sometime between April and June. Young cubs love to play. Some of their favourite games are wrestling with each other and chasing each other. They also have great fun playing tug-of-war.

Exercise 111 (Word Skills)

Homonym Crossword

Remember that homonyms are words that sound similar but do not have the same meaning. Look up any unfamiliar words in the dictionary.

Across

3. through
5. ate
7. ruff
10. hours
12. shoe
13. write
14. or, ore
15. oar, ore
16. weather
20. thrown
21. ale
22. roe
25. ad
27. night
28. sew, sow
30. sun
32. fir
33. our
34. won
36. know
37. oh
38. meat
39. dew, due
40. horse
42. pa
44. wee
45. urn

Down

1. hire
2. threw
3. taught
4. where
6. too, two
8. groan
9. high
10. owe
11. sore
17. heard
18. hoe
19. hi
23. byte
24. four
26. doe
27. nose
28. Sunday
29. throne
31. knot
35. knead
36. gnus
37. oar, or
38. main
41. hour
43. whacks

UNIT
30

Exercise 112 (Sentence Construction)

Correcting Run-on Sentences

A **run-on sentence** is two complete sentences jammed together.

EXAMPLE: My father didn't care much for cats he had always wanted a dog.

Here are three ways to correct run-on sentences.
1. Divide them into two separate sentences.

EXAMPLE: My father didn't much care for cats. He had always wanted a dog.

2. Separate the two parts of the run-on sentence with a semicolon.

EXAMPLE: My father didn't care much for cats; he had always wanted a dog.

3. Join the two parts with a coordinating conjunction to form a compound sentence.

EXAMPLE: My father didn't care much for cats, but he had always wanted a dog.

A. One of the following sentences is correct. Three are run-ons. Place a period at the end of the first sentence in each run-on. Cross out the first letter of the second sentence, and write the capital letter above it.

1. The girls on our school volleyball team lost their first three games they won their last five.

2. Don't move the ambulance will be here any minute.

3. The teacher was upset because Mark had not finished his homework.

4. At ten o'clock my grandfather decided to leave he was tired of waiting.

B. In the following paragraph underline any sentences that are fragments or run-ons.

The most useful of all the desert animals is the camel. During sandstorms the camel closes its eyes and nostrils broad pads on its feet keep it from sinking in the sand. If a camel does not eat for several days. It can live on food stored in its hump. The camel can find food where other animals would starve the camel's lips and tongue are so tough that it can eat plants with sharp thorns. If food is difficult to find, a camel will eat anything, including its owner's tent.

Now rewrite the paragraph in your notebook. Join the fragments to other sentences. Be sure to divide the run-ons into separate sentences.

A. Punctuate the following sentences correctly. Draw a line through each lower-case letter that should be a capital. Write the capital letter above it.

1. didnt mr goldberg say to study chapter 9 water and living things for tomorrows test asked jean

2. lets get out of here now shouted natalie

3. instantly lee jumped to his feet and asked who told you that

4. nicholas shrugged and then replied well its up to you

5. the tail pipe in my opinion should be replaced replied the mechanic

6. are you sure asked laura that you may open that cupboard

7. did you know that james naismith a school teacher in southern ontario invented the game of basketball in 1891 asked michael

8. the meeting at glendale school starts at eight oclock however we wont be there until later

B. In each of the following sentences circle the form of the pronoun that would be used in formal writing.

1. Did Steven and (she, her) get the highest marks on the math test?

2. The last two pieces of cake are for Noriko and (he, him).

3. After the race we saw Chris and (he, him) slowly walking home.

4. Scott and (she, her) climbed to the top of Mt. Arrowsmith last Saturday.

5. Did you get a birthday present from Olivia and (she, her)?

6. Mr. Soltani took Lorenzo and (he, him) to the hockey game.

7. I want to go swimming with Crystal and (they, them) before dinner.

8. Mr. Yamanaka divided the money between Saskia and (they, them).

9. Mrs. Bronstein drove the cheerleaders and (we, us) to the final game.

C. In the blanks, tell whether each sentence is simple, compound, or complex.

1. Insects have six legs, but spiders have eight. _____

2. A hummingbird can fly forward,
   backward, up, down, and sideways. _____

3. Unless I set the alarm, I probably won't
   wake up in time to go fishing tomorrow. _____

4. Giant pandas live mainly on bamboo; however,
   sometimes they eat other kinds of plants. _____

5. As far as I know, the final soccer game
   will be played on Saturday morning. _____

6. Peter and Shane always meet each other at
   the bus stop and walk to school together. _____

7. Please turn the volume down on the television
   or you'll wake the baby. _____

8. Because I lost the baseball, I have to pay for it. _____

D. Combine each pair of sentences into a complex sentence. Use commas where needed.

1. Jonathan ran to the door. He heard the siren.

   _____

2. Tiffany broke her ankle last week. She will not be able to play hockey for at least a month.

   _____

   _____

3. I won't be finished my homework until eight o'clock. You'll have to go to the concert without me.

   _____

   _____

afraid   anxious, cowardly, horrified, fearful, frightened, nervous, scared, terrified, troubled, uneasy

angry   annoyed, aroused, cross, enraged, furious, in a rage, inflamed, infuriated, irate, peeved

ask   demand, inquire, question, quiz, request

bad   awful, evil, horrible, naughty, rotten, spoiled, unfavourable, unpleasant, wicked, wrong

beautiful   attractive, charming, dazzling, desirable, elegant, gorgeous, handsome, lovely, magnificent, pretty, sparkling, splendid, stunning

begin   commence, inaugurate, launch, start

big   colossal, enormous, gigantic, great, huge, immense, jumbo, large, mammoth, massive, titanic, vast

brave   bold, courageous, daring, fearless, gallant, heroic, unafraid, valiant

break   burst, crack, crush, damage, destroy, shatter, smash, split, wreck

bright   brilliant, colourful, dazzling, gleaming, glittering, glowing, shimmering, shiny, sparkling

call   bellow, cry, roar, scream, whisper, yell

catch   capture, grab, hook, rope, snare, snatch

cool   bitter, chilly, cold, freezing, frigid, frosty, ice-cold, icy, unheated, wintry

cry   bawl, bellow, exclaim, howl, roar, scream, shout, sob, wail, weep, yell

cut   carve, chop, clip, saw, slash, slice, snip

dark   black, dim, dismal, dreary, gloomy, murky, shadowy, sunless

delicious   appetizing, enjoyable, juicy, luscious, scrumptious, succulent, tasty

dirty   dingy, dusty, filthy, grimy, messy, smudged, soiled, unwashed

dull   boring, dreary, humdrum, tedious, tiring, uninteresting

eat   bite, chew, crunch, devour, feast on, gobble, gnaw, graze, grind, gulp, munch, nibble, swallow

fall   collapse, dive, drop, plunge, sink, topple, tumble

fast   fleet, hasty, prompt, quick, rapid, speedy, swift

fat	chubby, obese, overweight, plump, pudgy, stout
full	crammed, crowded, heaping, jammed, loaded, overflowing, packed, stuffed
get	acquire, collect, earn, find, gather, obtain
good	agreeable, excellent, fine, first-rate, marvellous, pleasant, reliable, satisfactory, splendid, superb, superior, well-behaved, wonderful, trustworthy
happy	cheerful, contented, delighted, glad, jolly, joyful, jubilant, merry, overjoyed, pleased, satisfied.
hate	abhor, despise, detest, disapprove, dislike, loathe
hit	collide, crash into, pound, punch, run into, slam into, smash into, strike
hot	baked, boiling, burning, fiery, roasting, scalded, scorched, sizzling, steaming, sunny, tropical, warm
hurry	accelerate, bustle, dart, dash, flash, hasten, hustle, race, run, rush, speed, zip, zoom
important	essential, famous, indispensable, influential, necessary, outstanding, prominent, significant, substantial, valuable, well-known
interesting	absorbing, appealing, amusing, arousing, attractive, engrossing, entertaining, enthralling, exciting, fascinating, gripping, intriguing, spellbinding, thrilling
kind	considerate, friendly, generous, gentle, helpful, pleasant, thoughtful, warm-hearted
little	dwarfish, miniature, minute, pigmy, small, tiny, wee
look	explore, gape, gawk, glance, glare, glimpse, hunt, inspect, observe, peek, peep, peer, search for, stare, study, watch
mad	angry, annoyed, cross, disagreeable, enraged, furious, raging
make	assemble, build, construct, create, develop, fashion, invent, manufacture, produce
move	amble, bound, climb, crawl, creep, dart, dash, gallop, hobble, jog, paddle, race, ride, run, rush, saunter, scamper, scramble, scurry, shuffle, slide, slither, stagger, streak, stride, swagger, tear, toddle, trot, waddle, walk
new	current, modern, recent, unused
old	aged, ancient, antique, elderly, feeble
right	accurate, correct, exact, perfect, true

sad	dejected, depressed, gloomy, miserable, sorrowful, sorry, unhappy
say	admit, announce, argue, assert, boast, chat, claim, comment, complain, continue, discuss, explain, express, growl, grumble, insist, mention, mumble, mutter, note, order, promise, recall, remark, reply, snap, suggest, thunder, urge, whisper, yell
show	demonstrate, disclose, explain, guide, point out, teach
slowly	gradually, lazily, leisurely, sluggishly, unhurriedly
smart	bright, brilliant, clever, intellectual, intelligent, wise
stop	block, cease, conclude, discontinue, end, halt, prevent
strange	astonishing, extraordinary, fantastic, odd, peculiar, queer, unusual, weird
strong	forceful, mighty, muscular, powerful, rugged, sturdy, tough
take	capture, carry off, grab, kidnap, obtain, pick up, seize, snap up, snatch
thin	lean, scrawny, skinny, slender, slim
true	accurate, actual, authentic, correct, exact, genuine, real, right
ugly	hideous, repulsive, unattractive, unsightly
unhappy	cheerless, dejected, depressed, discontented, discouraged, gloomy, heartbroken, miserable, sad, sorrowful
walk	file, hike, limp, march, pace, prance, stagger, stalk, stamp, stride, stroll, strut, stumble, tiptoe, trudge, waddle
wet	damp, drenched, humid, moist, rainy, soaked, sodden, soggy, watery
wonderful	amazing, delightful, enjoyable, fabulous, fantastic, marvellous, spectacular, superb
worried	agitated, anxious, concerned, disturbed, troubled, upset
wrong	false, inaccurate, incorrect, unsuitable, untrue

INDEX

Adjective phrases, 109, 113
Adjectives
    definition, 74
    irregular, 100
    usage, 75
Adverb phrases, 110
Adverbs, 114
    definition, 84
    irregular, 100
    -ly construction, 86
    position in sentence, 87
    usage, 85, 88
Alphabetical order, 8, 26
Animal names, 5
Antecedents, 54, 58, 59
Antonyms, 53
Apostrophes
    with contractions, 92, 102
    with possessives, 93, 102
Appositives, 51
    combining ideas with, 45
    definition, 44
Audience, writing for, 106

Bibliography, 127
Body
    of letter, 106
    of report, 126
Business letters, 106

Capitalization, 7, 10, 25, 135
Classifying, 1
Clauses, dependent, 129
Clichés, 131
Closing, of letter, 106
Commas, 52, 77, 135
    with addresses, 27
    with appositives, 44
    with dates, 27
    with direct address, 39
    with interrupters, 39
    with series, 32
Comparatives, 98, 100, 114
Composition types
    descriptions, 94, 104
    letters, 106, 108
    opinion, 108
    reports, 123, 124, 126
Compounds
    predicates, 42, 56, 78
    pronouns and, 71
    sentences, 121
    subject, 42, 56, 70, 78
Conclusions, writing, 126
Confusing words, 73, 78, 79
Conjunctions
    co-ordinating, 120
    subordinating, 128
Contractions, 92, 102
Conversations, writing, 80

Descriptions, writing, 94, 104
Dialogue. see Conversations
Dictionary
    definitions, 34

entry words, 8
guide words, 9
pronunciation key, 18
Directions, following and giving, 33

Editing, 29, 76
Entry words, 8
Examples, explaining with, 43

Good/Well, 89, 113
Greek roots, 116
Guide words, 9

Heading, of letter, 106
Homonyms, 50, 69, 133

Index, using, 37
Introductions, writing, 126

Latin roots, 116
Lay/Lie, 101, 113
Letters
    business, 106
    opinion, 108
Lie/Lay, 101, 113

Main ideas, 11
Metaphors, 40

Notes, taking, 123
Nouns, 26
    agreement with verbs, 64
    collective, 6
    common, 6
    definition, 3
    proper, 6
    singular and plural, 12, 13, 19

Opinion, writing, 108
Order, within paragraphs, 38, 48, 104
Outlines, 124

Paragraphs
    definition, 11
    descriptive, 94, 104
    developing with details, 22
    developing with examples, 43
    developing with reasons, 48
    order, 38, 48, 104
    unity, 17, 25
Participles, 46, 47, 55
Personification, 40
Phrases, 103, 109, 110
Plot, 66
Possessives, 93, 102, 113
Predicates
    compound, 42
    definition, 30
    noun-verb agreement, 64
    position in sentence, 31
Prefixes, 57, 62, 63
Prepositional phrases, 103, 109, 111, 113

Prepositions, 103
Pronouns, 135
    agreement with nouns, 58
    antecedents and, 59
    compound subjects and, 71
    definition, 54
    object, 115, 118, 119
    subject, 112, 119
Pronunciation keys, 18

Quotation marks, 77, 135
    with exact words, 60
    with punctuation marks, 61
    with titles, 82

Reports, 123, 124, 126
Research, 123
Root words, 57, 83, 90, 91, 97, 114, 116

Salutation, 106
Semicolon, 122
Sentences
    combining, 45, 56, 111, 132
    complex, 130, 136
    compound, 121, 136
    definition, 4
    fragments, 4
    incomplete, 4
    run-on, 134
Signature, 106
Similes, 40
Story construction
    plot, 66
    time order, 65
    writing, 67
Subjects
    compound, 42, 56, 70, 78
    definition, 30
    noun–verb agreement, 64
    position in sentence, 31, 51
Suffixes, 90, 91, 97, 114
    definition, 83
Superlatives, 98, 100, 114
Syllables, 16, 52
Synonyms, 20

Table of contents, using, 36
Tenses, 35, 46, 47, 52, 55
Thesaurus, usage, 24
Time order, 38, 65
Topic sentences, 14, 25, 48

Verbs, 26, 77
    agreement with nouns, 64
    choosing, 72
    definition, 21
    helping, 28
    irregular, 46, 47, 55
    tense, 35, 46, 47, 52, 55
    usage, 88

Well/Good, 89, 113